CAREER BREAK COMPASS

CAREER BREAK COMPASS

Navigating your Path to a Balanced
Life Through Intentional Time Off

LAURA NGUYEN

THE
collective
BOOK STUDIO

Library of Congress Cataloging-in-Publication Data available.
ISBN: 978-1-68555-732-4
Ebook ISBN: 978-1-68555-862-8
Library of Congress Control Number: 2024901406

Printed using Forest Stewardship Council certified stock from sustainably managed forests.

Manufactured in China.
Design by Andrea Kelly.
Typesetting by Westchester Publishing Services

10 9 8 7 6 5 4 3 2 1

The Collective Book Studio®
Oakland, California
www.thecollectivebook.studio

To my daughter, for inspiring a renewed purpose within me.
To my wife, who continues to support my journey and evolution.
To my parents, for braving the dark seas to bring hope and love.

Contents

Introduction

When was the last time you actually took some time for yourself? I'm not talking about a hot bath with bubbles, although that's nice too. When was the last time you reconnected with you?

Did you spend your time as a kid going from school to activities, getting home only for bedtime? Today, are you the parent who finds yourself carpooling your way around town, from drop-off to pick-up to running errands?

You know the drill. You get up. Get the kids dressed. Get breakfast. Get in the car. School drop-off. Head to work. Start a day of nonstop meetings. Crap, it's 5:30. Time to go pick up the kids. Rush to the car. Drive to daycare. "How was your day, sweetie?" Rush home. Cook dinner. Rush out the door for 6:30 swimming lessons. Crap, forgot the goggles. Oh well. Check emails while sitting in the stands, waiting for the lesson to be over. Twenty-five more minutes. Scroll through Instagram. Time. Let's go to the locker room, shower, and head home. 8 p.m. Get the kids ready for bed. 9:30 p.m. Collapse on the sofa. 10:17 p.m. You hear the sound of little footsteps. "Mom, I'm hungry." F*ck.

This is our lives. Day in and day out.

It is exhausting, but it's just the way life is supposed to be. Right?

In November 2022, I left my VP corporate role. I left with no job lined up. I left a lot of money on the table. It was risky.

But the risks of staying? It's quite a list.

o Degrading mental health

o Plummeting physical health

- Having zero energy for the people I love

- Living my life by someone else's plan

- Being at the mercy of a need for validation

And honestly, I was incredibly unhappy on the inside, but smiling on the outside. The distance and time I gained from leaving my job gave me clarity on what I truly wanted in life:

- To laugh with friends and family

- To spend time with my spouse

- To get up and travel whenever I want

- To experience my kids' childhood with them

- To have the choice of doing what serves me

- To work on projects with people that fill my soul

And I had to say no to everything else. Life is extremely fragile and I realized that now was the time for change.

I learned that by creating a plan to re-evaluate my values and passions, I could take an *intentional* step to live a life that was my own.

And you can too.

Chart Your Course

I wrote this book to be a guide for those who are planning a career break. There are many types of breaks that can be taken, and my objective is to share with you a how-to guide to plan your break to maximize its impact on your life.

This book is broken into three parts. The first is the prep work, the second is how to structure your break to make the most of your time off, and the third is how to reintegrate to the work world and live more intentionally once your break is over.

As part of writing this book, I interviewed more than one hundred people to better understand burnout, how they were dealing with it, and how a career break benefited them. As a certified coach, I also work with clients to help them navigate finding balance as they struggle with burnout. Throughout this book, I will share their stories. All are anonymized to maintain confidentiality and respect their privacy.

Part 1

Decision-Making and Preparation

CHAPTER 1

Waypoint: How Did I Get Here?

"Water always goes where it wants to go, and nothing,
in the end, can stand against it.
Water is patient. Dripping water wears away a stone."

—*Margaret Atwood*

Water is the most powerful element. It can move around any obstacle without losing its essential nature. It is the most versatile element, with the ability to take on different forms— a solid, a liquid, a gas. It can dissolve mountains. It can destroy and it can bring life. Water can bring relief in the desert and it can drown you. For me, water has always symbolized a sense of renewal and transformation.

Think about famous stories involving the ocean. You'll probably think of your high school reading list:

- Homer's *Odyssey*, in which Odysseus journeys home by ship after the Trojan war.

- Virginia Woolf's *To the Lighthouse*, in which water plays so many symbolic roles.

- Jules Verne's *Twenty Thousand Leagues Under the Sea*, about Professor Aronnax and Captain Nemo on their exploration of the ocean depths.

- Yann Martel's *Life of Pi*, in which Pi Patel journeys on the ocean in a lifeboat with a Bengal tiger after a shipwreck.

- And even Hans Christian Andersen's *The Little Mermaid*, in which the mermaid princess longs for a life she doesn't have on land with a human prince.

What do all these stories have in common? They all speak to the allure, the mystery, and even the challenges of the sea.

Water and the sea have played a pivotal role in the story of my family. It is our past and our way forward.

My Story: How I Worked Myself into Burnout

I'm a daughter, sister, wife, mom, stepmom, mentor, and friend. I am the daughter of two Vietnamese refugees and a first-generation American achiever. I lived up to my parents' dreams and became a first-generation college and postgraduate degree holder. I graduated with two bachelor's degrees in three years and was my sorority's first Asian American lesbian president and the youngest person to graduate from my executive MBA program, in fifteen months with honors.

In the corporate world, I was promoted five times in three years, managed multimillion dollar accounts in my early twenties, and moved to executive roles by the time I was thirty. I have always been an achiever, and everywhere I went, I sought out opportunities to lead. Everything looked great on paper.

In 2017, I married my wife, Amber, and I became a stepmom to three kids, who are now twenty-three, twenty-two, and eleven. In April 2019, we welcomed Ellis, our beautiful and strong-willed daughter (may she keep that spirit forever). Despite having all the qualities I'd want her to have as a woman in this world, my headstrong, spirited daughter could be a challenge as a toddler. In the midst of the pandemic, like many parents, we kept her home and safe from exposure while trying to balance childcare, schooling, and both of our jobs. It was both a blessing and a nightmare. Our toddler had never slept through the night. I spent most nights waking up at least once or twice.

It should come as no surprise to anyone who has had young kids that with caregiving comes physical, mental, and emotional exhaustion. Everyone tells you how wonderful it is to bring a small human into the world, but they never tell you how truly hard it is. There is nothing to prepare you, and nothing comparable to the experience. The exhaustion from not sleeping starts when you're pregnant. At the time, I thought, "Oh, this is super uncomfortable." Fast-forward, and *discomfort* doesn't even begin to describe the level of exhaustion of raising a kid.

Then comes the mental and emotional exhaustion. You are constantly worried about keeping your little one alive, and then when they enter their toddler years, you are trying to keep yourself sane. Arguing with a toddler has to be worse than arguing with a narcissistic terrorist. There is no reasoning and often unsuccessful negotiating. And beyond barely surviving each day, you want to be an amazing parent who raises a happy, balanced, and productive future adult. You're dealing with the emotional trauma that you grew up with and trying to not repeat the cycle with your own child. It's just too much. As a parent to young children, this time is incredibly difficult in all aspects of life. But we also have two older children, and I'll say that it doesn't get easier, it's just different. Young adults in their early twenties have different needs from their parents. They are out in the world, making their mistakes, which requires you, as a parent, to have heightened levels of different anxieties and concerns.

At work, the pressure was just as intense, if not more so. I was achieving on the outside but struggling on the inside.

For three decades I have been a high achiever, frantically trying to climb a corporate ladder to prove to myself that I am enough—smart enough, good enough, worthy enough.

As VP of marketing, I was responsible for our company's growth and lead generation. It was a constant battle of not feeling good enough and wanting more, more, more.

When I had my daughter, I took twelve weeks maternity leave. When I returned, my team looked exhausted and unmotivated. Three months later, the resignation letters started to come in. By the end of the year, 30 percent of my team had resigned, all managers.

March 2020 hit all of us like a brick wall as the world struggled with a global pandemic. Stress levels were high, and lots of people started to evaluate their own mortality and priorities. I couldn't backfill the roles fast enough. And then 30 percent turned into 50 percent. By the summer of 2020, only three people had stayed.

The pressure kept piling on and I felt like a failure; I had failed my team and my organization, and the high turnover was the proof. Was it me? Was I just a terrible manager? Did I not know how to manage a team? This was the first time in my life I had lost so many direct reports. Despite their leaving, I was still in close contact with them as friends and we'd sometimes meet up for coffee. I'd ask for their candid feedback on where I went wrong, and they would answer, "It's not you, it was never you." Although that was good to hear, their responses didn't get to the bottom of it and didn't bring me comfort or ease.

I still had to answer to my boss, the CEO, and an executive team on why my department staff was dropping like flies. I had to show not only that could I continue to excel at my responsibilities, but also that none of my channels were suffering. It was suffocating, but I couldn't let the stress paralyze me. I stuck to my tried-and-true methods: smile, be solution-oriented, move faster, and look calm doing it.

Over time, I second-guessed myself, and imposter syndrome grew strong. I was in my head constantly—worried that I'd say the wrong thing and then get judged and penalized for it later. Would people say negative things about me? Would they say I wasn't good enough at my job? After twenty years in the corporate world, I felt anguish. I loved my job and I knew I was damn good at it, but somewhere I got lost. I couldn't breathe.

It's easy to blame circumstances for burnout. I wish I could say there was one final straw that made me quit my job. But here's the truth—it wasn't one decision. It was countless decisions I made over twenty years.

I wore these as badges of honor: I went nowhere without my laptop, I was early to work and stayed late. I lived on coffee and protein bars. I'd grind on weekends and vacations. I responded to every ping or notification. I'd take calls at 8:00 p.m., 10:00 p.m., or even 3:00 a.m.

But I did that at the cost of missing birthdays, dinners, family events, being late every day for daycare pickup, skipping anything resembling self-care, missing my daughter's first words. The list goes on and on. And then the reality of mortality hit when I experienced the sudden death of mentors and colleagues, of aunts and uncles.

That's when achieving stopped feeling good. It was replaced with emptiness and fear that I could lose what truly mattered for the sake of emails and forgettable projects.

From a physical perspective, I just didn't feel like me. I never lost the baby weight, and with the pandemic I ended up gaining another nineteen pounds on top of it. I felt tired, sluggish, and overall unhealthy. I was sitting at my desk all day. My Fitbit would scream at me because I'd get six hundred steps a day. I would joke, "I'm going to die." It was no joke.

My story is not unique. You're likely feeling some of this too. As you look around, you're overwhelmed. Your environment is chaos, your internal state is chaos, and your work is demanding and, yes, chaos. And yet, you probably feel guilty even complaining about your struggles. I felt that deep guilt too. I know that I should be grateful, and I am. I have a partner to help take on some of the load. Our family is healthy. We have good jobs that pay well. We have a roof over our heads. We should be grateful. You can be grateful and still know that there has to be more to life than work and this feeling of burnout.

My First Sailing

There was no denying that I felt aimless, and I was languishing. So I decided I needed to take a break. I took a weekend. I left the kids with my spouse, and I checked myself into a hotel down the road from our home. My goal was to "brainstorm" what my life's purpose was. I packed a stack of multicolored Post-it notes and a handful of Sharpies and sat in the hotel room alone trying to figure out what I needed to be happy. This was an exercise that I normally did annually, but this time, despite my attempts, I couldn't see beyond the blank sheet of paper.

The first three hours were extremely boring. The next six were even worse. I kept writing—one idea per Post-it note: What would I do if I wasn't worried about money? What would I do tomorrow if I knew I was going to die in six months? If I had $10 million in my bank account, what would I do? What matters to me? What legacy do I want to leave on this planet? I kept asking myself a series of questions, hoping to get to clarity, but instead I was blocked.

The truth was that my identity was shifting and that what was once important to me no longer mattered. How the hell did I get to this point? How did I get so lost? I have always been so certain.

Author and poet Brianna Wiest says, "If you really want to change your life, let yourself be consumed with rage: not toward others, not with the world, but within yourself." Well, I was mad as hell at where I was, that's for sure.

Climbing that corporate ladder now felt meaningless and unfulfilling. I just wanted to do great work with people I liked. And I wanted to raise my daughter to be joyful, in a world that would love and accept her. That's it. It was really that simple.

But those simple words were not so simple in execution. At least, at the time, I couldn't see it.

Although my job felt unfulfilling, it paid well and I needed to take care of my family. If I left that job, I'd just have to go get another one, so nothing would really change. I knew I wasn't stay-at-home-mom material—I wasn't a great teacher, and I lacked the patience required.

So what could I do? To say I was lost and overwhelmed would be an understatement. I began to realize that this was much deeper than typical exhaustion. My spirit felt broken, my soul felt sucked dry, and my body felt like mush.

I was walking around with a heavy weight on my shoulders, peering through my foggy brain and eyes, struggling with a permanent shortness of breath from the last panic attack and the fear of the next one coming. I was a walking zombie. I was desperate for anything that could bring me back to life again.

Until then, I had no idea just how much burnout could destroy you from the inside out—mentally, physically, and spiritually. I decided that if I was going to come back to life again, I had to find out everything I could about burnout— what it was and how to fight it. So I did what all responsible adults do: I went to Google and typed in "burnout cures."

What I learned kicked off my journey from burnout to balance and led me to discover the benefits of taking a career break. If you have ever felt anything like I did—read on.

Free Diving

In each chapter of this book, I've included exercises to help guide you along your journey as you prepare and plan for your career break. Much like free diving, where divers swim without heavy tanks and equipment, these exercises encourage you to navigate the depths with conscious decisions, self-awareness, and an acute understanding of your capabilities.

- When was the last time you felt truly alive, and what were you doing at that moment?

- Are there any habits or behaviors that are holding you back from reaching your full potential? How can you break or change them?

- In the Resources section (page 225), you'll find a template for a balanced life wheel. Complete it.

- Review your balanced life wheel (downloadable). Are there areas you'd like to improve, change, deprioritize?

- If you could achieve anything in life without the fear of failure or judgment, what would you pursue?

 SCAN QR CODE FOR DOWNLOADABLE ACTIVITY
Visit www.careerbreakcompass.com

CHAPTER 2

Learning the Ropes: Burnout 101

"When anxious, uneasy, and bad thoughts come, I go to the sea, and the sea drowns them out with its great wide sounds, cleanses me with its noise, and imposes a rhythm upon everything in me that is bewildered and confused."

—Rainer Maria Rilke

Before you try to leave burnout behind you and take to the open water, you need to learn the basics about burnout to understand the research.

Let's start with how the American Psychology Association defines *burnout*:

> *n.* physical, emotional, or mental exhaustion accompanied by decreased motivation, lowered performance, and negative attitudes toward oneself and others. **It results from performing at a high level until stress and tension, especially from extreme and prolonged physical or mental exertion or an overburdening workload, take their toll.**

Well, that doesn't sound great.

Since you picked up this book, you probably have an inkling that you have reached a point of burnout. But just in case you need a little more affirmation, complete the questionnaire on the next page.

If you answered yes to at least two of these questions, let me say that you're not alone. For so long, those of us feeling this way have said that it's just the way of life. We all work until we die. Maybe if we're lucky, we have some good years in retirement to enjoy our lives.

I believe the pandemic affected our way of thinking and believing. We were stuck at home, spending quality time with family, and we were scared. This fear sticks with you and makes you question what truly matters.

Why the Focus on Burnout?

Burnout is not a new topic. The term *burnout* was first coined by Dr. Herbert Freudenberger, an American psychologist, in the 1970s. Even prior to the COVID-19 pandemic, burnout was already an emerging concern for many countries. In fact, the World Health Organization (WHO) identified burnout

Burnout Questionnaire	Yes	No
Have you become cynical or critical at work?		
Do you drag yourself to work and have trouble getting started?		
Have you become irritable or impatient with others? Your family, spouse, coworkers, customers, or clients?		
Do you lack the energy to be consistently productive?		
Is it difficult to concentrate?		
Do you lack satisfaction from your achievements?		
Do you feel disillusioned about your job?		
Are you using food, drugs, or alcohol to feel better or numb yourself?		
Are you exhausted from not sleeping seven to eight hours a night?		
Are you experiencing unexplained headaches, stomach or bowel problems, or other physical complaints?		

as a global issue. So why are we all feeling the impact of it now?

I have a few ideas:

Pandemic Impact: The COVID-19 pandemic exacerbated burnout symptoms for many of us, and especially for healthcare workers. Those of us who were already struggling before went off the deep end with remote work, isolation, and caregiving responsibilities. The pandemic poured gasoline on our already smoldering issues.

Global Work Culture: The way we work isn't working. Today's work culture involves long working hours, high expectations, and the increasing use of technology, all of which have contributed to burnout. It's not isolated to the United States— it's prevalent in many countries and industries.

Economic and Social Factors: Economic pressures, job insecurity, and social expectations also contribute to burnout. The stress to hit revenue goals in a challenging economic environment trickles down. The fear of layoffs may have increased, but the actual rate of layoffs has not. In a review from the Bureau of Labor Statistics since 2002, there were two layoff peaks, the Great Recession in 2009 and then the pandemic peak in March 2020. The layoff levels between 2021 and 2023 have been consistently lower than in the preceding two decades.

Awareness and Reporting: More people are aware and talking about burnout. More research has emerged about burnout, and more people are seeking help for their experiences.

Driven by demanding work cultures, economic pressures, and the impact of the COVID-19 pandemic, burnout has become a pervasive issue across professions, industries, and countries. However, there's more to it. Burnout encompasses numerous facets of our life.

Types of Burnout

If you're like me, you're probably thinking about burnout as it relates to work. However, work is just one area of burnout that can negatively impact your life and your mental state. When I reflect on my own experience, work was a contributing factor, but it was the work coupled with parental burnout and relationship burnout that really made it debilitating.

———————

Think about all the jobs you have. No, really. All of them. All the unpaid jobs you engage in on a daily basis. We often joke that working parents have three shifts a day. The "get out the door" shift, "the typical workday" shift, and "the bedtime, dinner, and after-school activities" shift. Then you're probably logging back into work or feeling guilty if you don't. This isn't limited to those who are parents. We engage in different types of work each day. Caregiving for an aging parent? Volunteering? Professional development or networking? The side gig that you hope to be a full-time career at some point? The hobby you engage in that may or may not make money? We are multifaceted and multidimensional and so is our burnout.

As you map out the areas in your life where you feel burnout, it's important to recognize that this is a layered experience. There was not one singular reason driving you to pick up this book. So be sure that as you are reflecting on your needs, you also consider the feelings you need to acknowledge and the systems you need to put in place to reset, recharge, and rebalance your life.

Types of burnout:

- **Parental Burnout:** Do you have children you are caring for?

- **Caretaking:** Are you caring for an elderly person or family member?

- **Relationship:** Is your relationship with your significant other suffering? How about your relationship with your parents or family members? Do you have social connections?

- **Work:** How are you feeling about work? Are you feeling overstimulated and stressed? Undervalued?

Work Burnout

Dr. Barry Farber studied work-related burnout and categorized it into three areas: overload, being under-challenged, and neglect. You can feel overload burnout in caretaking, or neglect in relationships, and so on. Farber's categories can also be used to think about burnout in other areas of our lives.

Overload Burnout

Overload burnout is the most common type of burnout and what most people think of when they think of the topic. This occurs when people work harder to achieve success, often sacrificing their personal lives and health.

Signs you experience overload burnout:

- You say, "I am so overwhelmed and exhausted."

- You work fifty, sixty, or more hours a week.

- You find yourself venting about your stress, which then puts the people you care about into problem-solving mode and creating more stress and responsibility.

- You feel exhausted from caretaking, on top of your work, side gig, meal prepping, laundry, and all the million other household things.

- Your health begins to fail, you barely get to eight hundred steps a day, and you stop going to the gym.

Under-Challenged Burnout

Under-challenged burnout is when someone feels unmotivated because they aren't challenged or stimulated by the work they do. These are individuals who don't feel appreciated by their managers or superiors or the relationships in their lives. These individuals may feel a loss of passion for their work and don't feel fulfilled.

Signs you experience underchallenged burnout:

- You don't feel connected to your work, coworkers, or leadership.

- You feel disengaged and stuck in your role or even your life.

- You feel that you have unused skills and are wasting your time.

- You feel negative and cynical.

These individuals have passion, desire, and potential. Yet their existing roles and situations don't allow them to truly express themselves, and thus they cannot contribute their unique gifts.

Neglect Burnout

Neglect burnout happens when someone isn't provided with guidance and is left to their own devices. This will often leave them feeling helpless, frustrated, and anxiety-filled. These individuals start to experience negative self-talk, convincing themselves they are incompetent.

Signs you experience neglect burnout:

- You feel unmotivated.

- You feel like you cannot keep up with demands because expectations are not defined.

To me, not giving someone the dedicated time and attention to set them up for success is worse than the sink-or-swim concept. Yes, this can be a result of bad managers. However, this may also sound familiar in our personal lives, with our kids, and even with our spouses when we don't prioritize the time to check in, talk about where we want a relationship to go, or even have kind conversations about how someone's day went. All these lead to feeling neglected. And neglect has deep psychological impacts.

Personality Types Prone to Burnout

Burnout is both internal and external. For me, there was a predisposition to burnout based on my own internal insecurities. Put me in an environment that allows that insecurity and self-doubt to manifest and grow rampant, and I'm done for. The work has to start with you.

So who is typically more prone to burnout? Christina Maslach, psychology professor emerita at UC Berkeley, created the Maslach Burnout Inventory, a study that assessed burnout and found that it consists of related but separate dimensions, including emotional exhaustion, depersonalization, and a reduced feeling of personal accomplishment. Personalities more prone to burnout are those who lean more toward introversion and neuroticism. Neuroticism, one of the Big Five personality traits, is defined as a tendency to experience anxiety, depression, and self-doubt. This may result in frustration because there is a fear about performing at high levels, which then leads to isolation that further drives feelings of anxiety.

In short, these personality types are most prone to burnout:

- Introverts

- Perfectionists

- Type A personalities with a high need for control

- Those who are highly sensitive

- People pleasers

Wait, so people who are more introverted and neurotic are more prone to burnout? Cool. I feel a little called out here. However, it's not just these personality traits that lead to burnout. According to burnout researchers Michael P. Leiter and Christina Maslach, these environmental elements also foster burnout:

o High workload

o Lack of control

o Not being rewarded or being underpaid for the work

o Lack of community, and limited or no relationships at work

o Feeling a lack of fairness, trust, respect, and openness

o Not feeling psychologically safe

o Conflict with the organization's values

The more I read about burnout, the more I felt I was reading an autobiography:

o Being thrown a million tasks with no priorities.

o Never-ending work tasks. Feeling like I was drowning.

o Not having real friends at work. Feeling desperately alone.

o Not feeling I could truly share my perspective without judgment.

o Making good money but somehow feeling negative and unmotivated.

So, I get it, I was burnt. Like, crispy, well-done bacon. So what the hell was I supposed to do? I cannot tell you the amount of reading I did on mindfulness, resting (a.k.a. sleeping), and breathing. But every time someone would talk to me about these things, I wanted to hurl something at them. How was I supposed to rest when I had a two-year-old? How was I supposed to get eight hours of sleep, when I hadn't slept since 2018, and to be honest, I was an insomniac before that. My mind never slowed down, and a part of me was prideful about it. I liked being ten steps ahead of everyone else. But the achiever in me, I'd later find out, was just the people pleaser in me.

People Pleasing and Burnout

I am a card-carrying member of the people pleasers club. People pleasers are often susceptible to burnout because we have a hard time saying no. We don't like to let people down, so we take on tough projects to ensure that we are liked. People pleasers tend to get an F in boundary setting and instead attract people who will likely push our boundaries.

Have you heard Luisa's song from *Encanto*? When I heard it, it hit me like a gut punch. "I'm pretty sure I'm worthless if I can't be of service." Yes, Luisa, I feel you, sister. Who am I if I'm not that person for people? Who am I?

I'm not going to lie to you. I was deep in all the shit. I didn't know what to do; I felt lost and powerless. Everything felt so wrong, but what did I have to complain about? I had a well-paying job and a good title for a company that did good for the world, I worked remotely, I have a comfortable home, a supportive spouse, a great family, and I was in decent health.). I shouldn't be complaining, I should be ecstatic. But I wasn't.

Stages of Burnout

You don't just arrive at burnout town. It's a slow journey. Think of it like a cross-country road trip.

Phase 1: The Honeymoon Phase

At first, you get in the car, with all your snacks and road trip music ready to go. You start the car, your tank is full, and your seat belt clicks in. You are energized and excited. You couldn't be more optimistic!

Phase 2: The Onset of Stress

Suddenly, it starts to rain. Except, it's not just raining, it's pouring. Stress builds, and you start to feel anxious. You can't see out your windshield as your wipers frantically try to push off the rain. Your optimism fades.

Phase 3: Entry to Chronic Stress

The rain isn't letting up, so you pull off at the next exit. You are stressed and exhausted from white-knuckling your steering wheel. You decide you're going to check into a nearby hotel to rest for the night.

Phase 4: Burnout

Unfortunately, the only option is a one-star hotel that looks like a scene from a horror movie. The bed is extremely uncomfortable. You're exhausted physically and mentally, and it feels as if this trip will never end.

Phase 5: Habitual Burnout

The next day, you get back in the car, filled with a foggy brain. Unmotivated and drained, you feel there's no end in sight. You start your car. The Check Engine light flashes on.

This is the road trip from hell. And unfortunately, this is how many of us feel in our lives. Running on fumes, exhausted, and yet, still feeling we have to keep pushing forward. The question to ask is, where are you even going? Is there actually a destination?

Then, what do you do when you see the Check Engine light? Do you keep going, or do you stop to find a mechanic? For many of us, we are overwhelmed by the day-to-day and we lose sight of the signs for a checkup. We neglect regular maintenance, and we suffer the consequences tenfold. Think about the little chip that's probably on your windshield right now. Are you going to leave it there, or call a company today to come fix it before winter comes and your entire windshield needs to be replaced?

Reflecting on the past twenty years, I could see that whenever I hit Phase 3 (Entry to Chronic Stress), I'd switch jobs. I would start driving in a different direction where it seemed less stormy, and a new adventure would await me at the Honeymoon phase. It would typically take me a year or two to get to Phase 3. I'd hover there for a bit, and then I'd leave.

But this time was a little different. With the pandemic and desire to stay in a company for a decent amount of time, I stayed longer than I usually would have, and that's when I found myself deep in Phase 5 (Habitual Burnout). Yes, it was likely accelerated by the pandemic, having a child, and other macro factors. But it didn't change the reality.

I've talked to many of my coaching clients about this, and like me, they kept driving right into Phase 5. They kept driving with the Check Engine light on. And now, the car is smoking on the side of a gravel road.

How Long Does Burnout Last?

This is a common question people ask me. Knowing the answer won't make you feel any better. It can be anywhere from six months to years for recovery. I kept thinking, is it like a breakup? I remember an episode of *Sex and the City* where Charlotte said that it takes half the amount of time of the relationship to get over it. So, if you've been burned out for five years, is recovery two and a half years? If you're burned out for eighteen years, does it take nine to dig yourself out of it? Are you kidding me?! Who has time for that?

At the moment you decide you need change over comfort, it's hard to continue denying the truth. Deep down, our bodies know. I basically had no immune system; exacerbated by not taking care of myself (and an adorable toddler who sneezes in my face), I was sick all the time. My body was constantly tense. I'd sit at my desk and feel my hamstrings tighten. (No, it didn't count as exercise. Darn!)

Over coffee recently, a friend (and former boss) shared an anecdote about being called out for looking visibly burned out. We've all probably experienced this at one time or another—a friend or colleague or even your hair stylist says to you, "You don't look like yourself. Your energy just seems low." It's hard denying you're burned out when the person you look at in the mirror has lost that spark.

So what's the solution? Just walk away? How do you keep your distance from burnout when you spend fifty-plus hours of your day in it? And you don't have nine years of free time to recover from it? We can't just quit our jobs and hang out on the beach. (Though, that does sound quite tempting. Sign me up!)

How to Recover from Burnout

In my experience, there are three ways to deal with burnout. First, you can ignore it, until it hits you like a freight train. Second, you can incorporate daily actions to help reduce its impacts. And, third, you can plan for and take an intentional career break.

Option 1: Denial

We aren't wired for prolonged discomfort and not being in control. Yet so many of us sit in denial until our health or relationships break down or the decision is made for us. Denying burnout will result in your body telling you that a break is needed. Or you may get laid off. Don't let yourself get stranded in the middle of the ocean without an oar. Plan for your career break so burnout doesn't break you.

Option 2: Small Actions Compound Over Time

It's easy to get into unhealthy habits where we aren't taking care of ourselves. You put yourself on the back burner. You don't prioritize yourself and your needs. For many people, small actions over time help. This means incorporating mini-breaks throughout the day to prioritize yourself and your health.

In their book *Burnout: The Secret to Unlocking the Stress Cycle*, Emily and Amelia Nagoski write about the need to reduce burnout by completing the stress cycle. The Nagoskis share that stress happens in a cycle that needs to be completed. Consider how our systems were created. If you were in the Serengeti just enjoying your environment and you hear a lion rustling in the field behind you, your senses would heighten. Then you'd sprint like hell. Once you get to safety, your heart rate would slow down, and you'd normalize. Your stress cycle closes and completes.

Today, we live in a heightened state of stress that doesn't complete. The Nagoskis share seven science-backed ways to complete that cycle.

1. Deep, slow diaphragmatic breathing

2. Positive social interactions

3. Movement/exercise

4. Laughter

5. Affection

6. Crying it out

7. Creative expression

These are powerful habits we should all incorporate into our lives. I knew all these things could work, but I also knew it was easier said than done. I would spend two weeks breathing, but then I'd get triggered by something at work and fall out of the habit. I would schedule coffee chats with friends but would end up canceling or I'd feel stressed that I needed to get back for a meeting. I'd laugh and cry. I couldn't even imagine having a hobby, but I tried those darned adult coloring books and it just left me with a cramped hand. As for affection, I was so depleted that I couldn't even imagine spending quality time with my spouse. I just didn't have any energy to give.

Instead of doing what I knew I needed to, I could go back to option 1 and dig in, dig deep, deep into denial, or I could do something different.

"JUST TAKE A BREAK. HOW ABOUT A VACATION?"

You've probably heard this, right? "Take some much-deserved time off." Believe me, I tried this. But you all know the truth: with easy access to the tools you need to work remotely, we are just working elsewhere when we're on vacation. I would go with my family on vacations and I'd duck away to make a call, prepare a presentation for next week's board meeting, or check in with my team and make sure that our leads were performing. It was always something.

Did someone ask me to log on? Sometimes, but not all the time. What kept me and a lot of other people I've talked to glued to our phones and laptops was ourselves. We felt the pull to check in. Maybe the feeling comes from some unspoken culture. Maybe it's from some side comment your boss made about being sure to check emails on the weekends. Or maybe it was just the need to feel, well, needed.

Option 3: Take the Career Break

The next option is to take a career break. Taking this break requires time and planning. You have to be intentional with this time to rest, reset, and recover. A career break takes diligent planning, and when you're exhausted, your brain can't get there. That's why I wrote this book—it's your guide to creating a plan. It doesn't have to feel unsurmountable and out of reach.

The reality is that burnout is not a singular issue, and simply taking a little time off will not cure it. Instead, we need to change our habits and become self-aware of our own impact.

Moving Forward

There are four paths for you to take.

Career Break: A career break is an extended time away from work that can be planned or unplanned. Unplanned breaks are common for those who were laid off. Whether by choice or circumstances, how you spend the time off is critical to healing and rebuilding your confidence. A career break can last anywhere from a couple of months to years. After a career break, you may go back to a similar role or industry, or pivot to a new path.

Sabbatical: A sabbatical program is an extended time away from work granted to an employee. Companies that offer sabbatical programs will define eligibility and program details. This can be for study, travel, or personal development. They can be paid or unpaid and range from four weeks to a month long. When your sabbatical is over, you go back to your job.

Leave of absence: The third path is a leave of absence. A leave of absence can be used to take care of health conditions, for caregiving of a child or aging parent, military leave, or other circumstances.

Roughly 30% of the people I've interviewed and worked with took a medical leave due to stress. This time off was anywhere from one month to six months leave. Many of those who took a leave of absence or medical leave returned to their jobs, even if for a transitional time before finding another role.

Regularly Scheduled Mini-Breaks: The final path is taking mini-breaks regularly. Research shows that the frequency of time off from work matters more than the duration. For you, this could mean treating your weekends like vacations, instead of a chance to catch up on laundry. Or you can regularly schedule your shorter vacations throughout the year, rather than one long vacation a year. In an interview with Shashank Nigam, CEO of the small aviation consultancy SimpliFlying, he shared his approach to addressing overwork at his organization. He instituted a mandatory one-week vacation for every eight weeks of work.

Which of these paths you choose depends on your circumstances, your personal and/or financial situation, your comfort zone, and other factors. For the sake of simplicity, I will use in this book the term *career break* to signify any kind of extended break from work beyond a vacation. The planning process for an extended amount of time off, what to do with your time off, and how to reintegrate are all applicable.

Normalize Breaks

Breaks are normal. Think of the three-month breaks you had each summer when you were in school or the three weeks off around the holidays in December and January. What about a gap year? These things are normal. If you're like me, you filled these extended breaks with summer courses, internships, or even full-time jobs. But being productive doesn't mean killing yourself. Success doesn't need to be an endless marathon. And besides, there is no medal at the end of the rat race. (I checked.)

Taking a sabbatical or career break can be an empowering and life-altering decision that allows you to engage in more meaningful self-reflection and exploration. There are a variety of reasons why people may choose to take extended time away from work. For some, it's about continuing self-development, learning a new skill, or finishing a project. For others, it's about exploring the world or immersing themselves into a service and volunteerism.

And then there's the rest of us who are just fried to a crisp and need to hit the reset button. (Hello, raising my hand.) You know total burnout pushed me to take a break. The purpose of taking a sabbatical or career break is to create distance between ourselves and our work environment, which allows us to refocus our energy in ways that will ultimately benefit us in the long term. This intentional time off also serves as an opportunity to evaluate career trajectories and realign our goals.

Mortality is also a teacher. I cannot tell you the number of people who told me that death was the catalyst for their career break. The sudden loss of a coworker, spouse, or family member forces us to take a deep look at ourselves and the choices we've made. Loss wakes us up to how short and precious life truly is, and in the process of our grieving we start to question whether what we're doing matters. And unfortunately, our companies' three-day bereavement policy isn't sufficient. A career break allows us to properly process our emotions and serves as a touchstone to re-evaluate our priorities and decide what changes are needed.

If you are like me, you probably know deep down that you need a break. And then the universe puts the wheels in motion. I read Tim Ferriss's *The 4-Hour Workweek*, I recalled mentors who took time off, and then my favorite podcasts started talking about breaks.

Jonathan Fields of *Good Life Project* and *Sparked* talked about how he was hesitant to take a pause, but after talking to Jenny Blake, the author of *Pivot*, he decided to take one month off. As an entrepreneur he needed to make plans to be sure that his organization would continue to run without him. During his sabbatical his goal was to work on a meaningful writing project.

Brené Brown shared that she would take three months off after a tough personal and professional season that included the failing health of her mother and the social media backlash she received from taking a pause from Spotify over issues regarding Joe Rogan's COVID misinformation on his podcast. In May 2022, Brown wrote, "I can't let that happen to me or to our organization. We need breath and space. To reinvest in that space, I've decided to take a sabbatical this summer."

Breath and space. That sounds like exactly what a lot of us need right now.

Different Types of Career Breaks

In the interviews I conducted, what emerged were four different types of career breaks. All these breaks provided a transformative experience, though different from one another.

Passion Projects. Those who take a career break to work on a passion project are making time to work on something personally meaningful. This could include writing a book, immersing themselves in art classes, or spending more time on their side gig. This may also include spending time on a community service initiative. Many may shift from full-time work to full-time project work. These individuals will have periods of rest, but the aim is to shift their focus for this time. They tend to go back to their old jobs.

Adventure. Adventurers are freedom-seeking travelers. Think taking a gap year to backpack or travel around the world. Adventurers tend to spend their time experiencing the world around them. Once their career break ends, many of them will return to their previous workplaces or find a very similar line of work.

Restful Recovery. Many of the people I talked to fall into this category. Resters take a career break because they need time away from work and seek healing, restful balance. This could be after a long sprint at a company or a natural transition. Those seeking restful recovery focus on self-care and personal priorities, such as their health or family. Their only agenda is to not work. Typically, they will find a role in a similar field.

Soul-Searching. This is another common category. This group hopes for some radical change by taking a career break. Soul-searchers and resters are those who experience deep exhaustion and burnout. They feel a career break is their last resort. The difference between soul-searchers and resters is that they feel their current path just doesn't work. They need to find something different. Searchers typically incorporate aspects of the other career breakers. They seek adventures and rest and integrate those practices into their lives.

It likely comes as no surprise that I was a soul-searcher. I approached my career break with two specific intentions: (1) to rest and recharge and (2) to prepare myself to create something I was passionate about. The issue was, I needed to do the first part to know what I wanted to do in the second part.

I knew that I wanted to do work that ignited me, made me feel I was making a meaningful contribution to the world, and made me a more joyful person, not only for myself, but also for my partner, my family, and the world. I needed to make a shift, but first I needed to recover from my burnout and exhaustion before I could figure out what my joyful future would look like.

Free Diving

- What type of career breaker do you most align with? When you think about taking a career break, what are three words that describe how you feel?

- In a table, list what you've done to manage your stress in column 1. In column 2, add the latest date you've completed each of those activities. In column 3, add what date you will commit to doing it again.

- Journal in response to the following prompts:

  - How would I spend an extended amount of time off of work?

  - What do I need to feel good about taking a career break?

- In what ways have you kept yourself on autopilot? In what ways have you ignored the Check Engine light?

- Is your personality type more prone to burnout? What attributes have you described as strengths that may also lead to burnout?

SCAN QR CODE FOR DOWNLOADABLE ACTIVITY
Visit **www.careerbreakcompass.com**

CHAPTER 3

Your Inner Compass

> *"The human heart is like a ship on a stormy sea driven about by winds blowing from all four corners of heaven."*
>
> —Martin Luther King Jr.

I am a firm believer that when we unravel all that society has layered onto us, we know what we want. Deep down, we know. The challenge in today's busy world is that we ignore all the signals and instead fight the current. Your inner compass is your guide to the direction you want to flow. Listen to it and follow it.

Your Body Knows: Listen

When I look back, there were many red flags about my high-achieving anxious behaviors. For the longest time, I thought that my ability to be ten steps ahead was my superpower. Today, I recognize that it was my anxiety fueling that need to be ahead, as a way to gain control of my surroundings. Our bodies give all of us these signals. It's the rash we get when we're stressed, it's our bitten-off nails, it's the headaches and migraines, and it's the stomach pains. It's time to listen to your body.

I remember my first real job out of college. I'd get to the office around 6:30 a.m. to work on my first client report. I'd power through the day, and sometimes head home around 6:00 p.m. for dinner, and then return to the office around 8:00 p.m. and work until 11:00 p.m. After that I'd head off to the bars with my friends, then start over the next day. Oh, to be young again. I was easily putting in fifteen-hour days, and I was a machine. I was promoted five times in three years, and I loved my job, my coworkers, the clients, all of it. A couple of years in, I started experiencing severe constipation and stomachaches. When the bleeding started, I waited six months before I went to the doctor. My doctor immediately referred me to a specialist, and at twenty-four years old, I had my first colonoscopy and endoscopy. No polyps, no cancer (thank god). Just IBS, triggered by stress and anxiety. I blamed the traveling and poor diet, told myself I'd find a more balanced job, and moved on to my next roles at different companies.

Fast forward, and I've had a board of advisors helping me achieve my career goals. Unfortunately, I had not paid attention to my body.

For nearly twenty years, my body was trying to tell me that I needed to take a deeper look inside and pay attention. I ignored the signs, even with a diagnosis from a professional and challenges that would pop up weekly.

I am not alone. Many of us are hurting inside, and that stress manifests itself in our bodies. Stress increases the release of cortisol, and that increased cortisol can have damaging impacts on the body, resulting in headaches, chest pain, insomnia, and increased blood pressure. Our bodies are telling us to watch out, to pay attention, to pause, to do something different. This is our Check Engine light.

In the interviews I've conducted, all shared a similar story of how their body reacted to stress. They would experience insomnia, constant fatigue, inflammation, unexplained pain, and frequent headaches. Our bodies were not intended to be in constant survival mode. A client shared that the turning point for him was his last annual physical. His blood pressure and cholesterol levels had increased, cortisol levels were extremely high, and he had frequent headaches. Sometimes, it takes this wakeup call to tell us that we need to do something different, and that we need to start prioritizing our health.

Your North Star

In the middle of the ocean, your ability to find the North Star is critical to your direction and survival. In this journey, you will need to clearly identify your career break "North Star" to ensure you can maximize your time off.

For me, the purpose of my break was to get clear and get aligned to who I am. I needed to give myself time and space to figure out myself again among the noise. The things that were important to me were to bring back creativity and rebuild myself from the inside out. I needed to answer some questions: What are my priorities? What do I want out of life? My "why" was to find my way to myself. Your "why" may be different, and it's important to set your intention for this time off and remind yourself of that reason early and often.

As you embark on this journey, you need a star statement of why you are doing this. It should be brief and something you'll remember when the questions come flooding in. When you flounder or veer off course, you will use this star statement to shine a light in the direction you need to go and remind yourself why your career break or time off matters.

Here are a few examples:

○ I need to take this time to take care of me, so that I can better care for my people.

○ I need to get my mojo back.

○ I want to take the time to reflect on my personal goals, values, and passions. It's essential for me to invest in self-discovery and grow on a personal level, so I can make informed decisions about my future career path.

○ I want to take this opportunity to recharge, relax, and engage in activities that bring me joy and fulfillment.

○ I want to prioritize my personal life, nurture my relationships, and pursue my personal interests and hobbies. I need to learn how to create a better balance between my professional and personal responsibilities.

○ I yearn to explore new interests, develop new skills, and gain diverse experiences. I want to dedicate this time to [time to learn a new language, acquire technical expertise, or pursue a passion project].

- o I need to focus on my healing journey, engage in therapy, practice mindfulness, and prioritize self-care for my well-being.

Most people react with horror and disbelief when you let them know that you are unsure what your next work chapter will be. For most, staying in a well-paying job is far better than facing uncertainty. They choose comfort. You will have to fight that tempting desire for comfort.

Society tells us that we should hustle and grind, and that this is the way of life. I believed this lie too. No more. All hustle and grind gave me were panic attacks and love handles. People may judge. Let them. Be honest with yourself and commit to how you want to live.

As you go through your career break, this North Star statement will evolve into a guide for the rest of your life. For now, let's start small and focus only on your North Star for the duration of your career break.

Your Limiting Beliefs: Let Them Go

When I first started talking about my struggles with burnout so publicly, people were shocked. How could I be so vulnerable? Then, when I started talking about taking a career break to help me reset and recover from burnout, the questions (and even the critics) got louder.

We talk about our stresses subtly. It's in passing that we'll vent to a friend or a coworker. You may have been stuck in this situation before. You have a terrible colleague or boss that just gets on your nerves. Ankle-biters, my friend used to call them, and then she would proceed to dance in the middle of our hallway as we walked to a meeting. I laughed, mostly because her dance moves were not stellar, and also because I felt the nibbles too. We'd sit and complain about not feeling supported, not having enough funding, how our clients just didn't get it. The list goes on.

Every good story has a hero, a victim, and a villain.

Think of the situations where you've been in one of these roles. How often were you the villain? Almost never, right? It's so easy to point fingers and blame someone else for your exhaustion and your burnout. It is this belief system that leads to our own undoing. However, when you're in that all-time-low moment, the moment on the bathroom floor crying, it isn't about blaming or shaming. That moment is about the truth—that something must change, that you must change.

This is why you picked up this book and why you are considering a career break. You know that deep down, you can't ignore the voice inside you anymore. You know that you need to refill, you just don't know how to do it.

- The first step is to take accountability and shift away from the blaming narrative and move toward an empowering one. Reframe how you think about the issue, and then take action. Do something different with the information you receive.

- "How did this happen to me?" becomes "What can I learn from the situation I am in now?"

- "There's no way out of this situation" becomes "What are the options? Who can I reach out to who would give me insights? Do I need to take a step away from the stimulus to decide?"

- "I'll never be able to catch my breath" becomes "What is my body telling me right now?"

- "I am a failure" becomes "Is that true? Where in my life have I proven to find solutions?"

All these reframed thoughts require us to pause before we emotionally react to our insecurities. In a lot of ways, pausing was the key to everything for me. In Tibetan Buddhism, there is a term, *bardo*, which means the state between death and rebirth, or gap, interval, intermediate state, or transitional process. It is the space in between. The steps I took before my career break and during my break are about *bardo*. I was giving myself permission to sit in this in-between space.

A Call for Connection

Over the past year, I have received emails and stories from people who have taken a much-needed break. When I started to openly share my journey on LinkedIn. My post about leaving my VP job to create more meaning and to give myself more choices and more memories reached more than 7 million people and received more than 53,000 engagements. I received more than 2,000 messages from people all over the world, from different levels in the work world, and they all had the same story. It resonated because there are so many of us feeling burned out.

I spent weeks poring over all the messages and comments. In the majority of the comments, people talked about how their mental health and physical health started to deteriorate over time. They realized that they were numbing their pain with food, alcohol, or endless scrolling. They were tired, not sleeping, and chronically stressed.

I see you. I get the exhaustion. You laugh off the memes of corporate America, of exhaustion and the cats clicking away at their computers. The passive-aggressiveness and resentment only increase. And slowly it all erodes your spirit and your soul. It did for me. What I missed so deeply was a community of people who saw me—of people who got it. When I first meet with new coaching clients, I'm 95 percent certain they will say this phrase: "This is the first time I'm talking about this to anyone." After hundreds of meetings, I am sad to say that often I'm right. And after hundreds of these calls, I still hold sadness and empathy for that statement, because I have deeply felt that loneliness too.

We are all suffering and looking for more connection. In the United States, half of adults reported experiencing measurable levels of loneliness. Loneliness is linked to increased risk of heart disease, stroke, and dementia. The General Social Survey of 2016 found that people are twice as likely to report that they are always exhausted compared to 20 years ago, and 50 percent of people across professions were burned out, and the more burned out, the lonelier they feel.

One of the key challenges of management and leadership is the loneliness that accompanies the role. Recent Gallup data shows that having a "best friend" at work has become increasingly important post-pandemic. Having friendships at work increases engagement, reduces turnover, and increases productivity. Personally, I was looking for connection and I felt very alone at work, which likely contributed to my burnout. Despite having a team and being in meetings all day, it was challenging to talk about stressors. I couldn't show weakness, I can handle anything! Bring me your stress, and I'll solve your problems. That's what the job entails, right?

The air grows thinner the higher you go up the corporate ladder. A survey of C-level executives in the United States, United Kingdom, Canada, and Australia reported that nearly 70 percent of C-suite executives were seriously considering quitting for a job that better supported their well-being. These executives said that improving their well-being was more important than advancement. It is not a question of *if* you will experience burnout, but *when* and *how* you will cope with it.

If you are seeking a connection with others who are interested in a career break, you'll find access to our online community in the Resources section (page 225).

Stories of Career Breakers

As a wave approaches shore, the front of the wave will slow, and the back overtakes the front, creating a crest that tumbles into a breaker. Similarly, for those on a career break, our forward-facing career slows, and the core us, what we've held back and delayed for so long, rushes forward. Throughout the book, I share stories of these incredible career breakers, making waves in their own lives. Here are a few.

Anna: The One Who Can Handle It

Anna tells the story we all know too well. She accepted the perfect-on-paper job. Two months in, she starts to experience constant neck pain and a loss of appetite. At first, she thought it was ergonomic issues. So, she made adjustments, but the truth was, her setup had not changed. Same desk, same chair. It wasn't that. It was the work culture she was in. Her work environment was toxic and hostile, and her body was showing signs of stress.

Anna had always prided herself as someone who could handle anything and everything. In fact, her boss noted in a performance review, "Anna has a get-the-job-done attitude." It was her badge of honor. She has a history of working with difficult personalities and demanding workplaces, but she had always adjusted. What made this time different? She said it may have been the pandemic shifting her perspective. Or maybe it was to set a better example for her kids. Or that she now knows her worth.

After six months in the role, she recognized that any identity she had built around being someone who doesn't give up wasn't worth it. She quit, her toxic workplace to give her time to reflect, reassess, and course correct. Today, Anna runs her own marketing consultancy practice.

Kumar: Clarity on the Circle of Life

I received this letter from Kumar that I thought would be helpful to share.

"I was at the top of my career and still had desires to achieve more. However, catching COVID in November of 2020 was a wakeup call for me; I lay on a couch for three weeks not knowing if I was going to make it. So, in the summer of 2021, I submitted my retirement paperwork. The strange thing was I felt like a zombie the whole time. I had no deep emotional feeling about it. Financially I was able to, so on paper it was okay.

I kept asking myself what was wrong with me. That's when I started Google searching burnout, and lo and behold, that was me. I was completely burnt. All COVID did was accelerate it. I was spent, my passion was gone, I did not care, etc., I was lost.

It took me three months to deprogram my body and mind from the day to day of work. Sunday evenings my mind would go into prep for the next day of work. I still was waking up at 4:30 a.m. even though I was no longer working and I had shut off all wake-up alarms. I found myself in a vegetative-like state.

I used to tell people and even my own kids that one had to keep the circle of life in balance or one gets in trouble. Circle of life: emotional, spiritual, and physical. If one of those is off-balance, it's not so bad. It's easy to recover. But if two or all three are out of whack, you're done. Burnout could affect all three areas and at once."

Kumar's story deeply resonated with me. Having a clear understanding of all the aspects that keep our life in balance is essential. We cannot over-index in work, and have it eclipse our life. We often find ourselves on auto-pilot, aimlessly drifting through life believing things are just okay. You know deep down there's more to life than just okay. An intentional break is just the beginning of living an intentional life.

Free Diving

- Why do you want to take a career break? Truly and deeply, what is your driving reason for this time off?

- Write down your anti-goals. What do you never want to do?

- Write down your North Star statement. What will you go back to when you waver?

- When you are presented with returning to your same workplace or making a career transition, where do you lean, and why?

 SCAN QR CODE FOR DOWNLOADABLE ACTIVITY
Visit www.careerbreakcompass.com

CHAPTER 4

Preparing for Rough Seas

"For whatever we lose (like a you or a me),
it's always our self we find in the sea."

—E. E. Cummings

We make thirty-five thousand choices a day. We choose what time we wake up, if we are going to actually get out of bed, what we're going to wear, what we're going to eat for breakfast, what shoes to put on before we walk out of the house, if we're going to run that red light. We make all these choices (and many more) before 8:00 a.m.

Choosing to stay in a role that doesn't fulfill you is also an active choice. When we skip the gym to join a lunch meeting, we are choosing to prioritize work over our health. When we check our email instead of being present with our family, we are choosing work over people we love. When we don't set and communicate our boundaries, we are choosing to deprioritize ourselves.

We are not powerless in our life. That is something that took me a while to figure out. For so long, I had believed that I was living in the prison that corporate America had built for me. Just keep achieving and I'll be good enough. Just be good, and I'll be rewarded. Just deal with it because that's what we are supposed to do. What I failed to truly understand until now is that the door was never locked. I just didn't try to open it and leave.

The important thing to remember is that time is a gift. Surviving in a high-fear state of mind is not living. Yet we are stuck because of fear.

In the interviews I've conducted and clients I've worked with, there are common fears that start to rise to the surface. The anxiety starts to creep in when considering a career break, and they may sound like this:

Fear of failure. What if I totally screw this up? What if I suck and I'm not actually that smart? What if my new ventures fail and I cannot provide for my family? I can't do what I want because I have responsibilities. What am I if I cannot provide for my family?

Fear of rejection. What if my family rejects me? What if I can't get another job because I have a career gap? What if it makes me unemployable? What if my friends and network turn away from me because I lost my way?

Fear of judgment. What will people think of me? What if I can't do this? Who do I think I am to even deserve this sabbatical? I'm not special. I should just get back to work and prove that I am good enough! What will my family think of me? What will my boss think? What does my company think? What do my mentors think? Will they think that I lost my mind and had a mental breakdown?

Fear of worthiness. Who am I to deserve this time? How can I be so selfish? What makes me so special? My family came here from another country for me to have a better life. Am I seriously opting out and walking away from the table because I am tired?

Fear of being overlooked or forgotten. What if I'm just insignificant? What if people forget I even exist? What if they just don't appreciate everything I've done for them?

Fear of succeeding. What if I do succeed, will it last or will it be fleeting? How much will change if this does happen? What if it's just a fluke?

Fear of the unknown. What's on the other side of this? Who will I become? What if I figure out in all this self-exploration that I need to burn it all down and start over? What if I need to make a huge change?

Our fears tend to go from zero to a hundred in sixty seconds. You'll force your family to live on the streets, you'll be starving, you'll never get another job. Is that true? Like, really though? Wouldn't you find a way to survive if you really needed to? What it all boils down to is the critic. It was the inner critic and negative self-talk, not the opinions of other people.

Don't Panic

Those in this high-fear state of mind are operating out of a fight, flight, freeze, fawn, or flop response. When the panic sets in, people will respond in different ways. Here are a few ways these responses manifest when related to burnout and career breaks:

- **Fight:** The fight trauma response involves a release of hormones (primarily cortisol and adrenaline) that triggers a reaction to "fight" the threat. A healthy fight response is setting boundaries and advocating for yourself. An unhealthy fight response is rage quitting.

- **Flight:** Our stress hormones are released and it signals us to flee. In this situation, we are frantically searching on job boards for any roles we might remotely be qualified for. In many cases, this will get us back into the same situation we were in before or in some cases a worse situation. A phrase I often use with clients is, "Are you running away from your old job, or aimlessly running toward a new one?"

- **Freeze:** The freeze response leaves us paralyzed by fear and unable to move. We may feel numb or a sense of dread. We are physically there but not mentally or emotionally present.

- **Fawn:** The fawn response is an act of compliance. It often occurs after you've tried fight, flight, or freeze responses several times without success. This often manifests into people pleasing, and you may disregard your own happiness and well-being.

- **Flop:** Flop occurs when you become entirely physically or mentally unresponsive and may even faint. Fainting as a result of fear is caused when someone gets so overwhelmed by the stress that they physically collapse.

In high-stress environments, each of these responses is intended to help you survive a bear attack, not your day-to-day work and life. So, whether you make the decision to plan a career break, or the decision is made for you, the key is to be thoughtful about how you approach this time. Use it to create a plan that allows you to recharge, gain clarity, and define what you want to do next for a more integrated life and career balance.

When I made the decision to take a career break from the hustle and grind, I knew it was against the very fabric of my being. I knew that it went against all of my conditioning. Work hard and keep working hard. My immigrant family's mantra was to create a better life in America. However, what I also knew was that the prison I had built for myself had to also be undone by me.

Martin Seligman is the father of positive psychology, and he is famous for a study he conducted with dogs in 1977. In the study, the research team built a shocking floor on one side, and a regular floor on the other. In between, there was a partitioning divider. First, they kept the partition low and put the dog inside. When the shocking floor was turned on, the dog would jump over the low partitioned divider to the normal, safe side. Then, they moved the partition up the wall, making it so that the dogs could not flee the shocking floor. Initially, the dogs would frantically try to escape, but when they realized they couldn't, they just lay on the shocking floor. This is what Seligman coined *learned helplessness*. The dogs did not continue to fight to escape, despite being shocked. Instead, they just lay there, continuously being shocked.

How many of us are living this kind of life? We feel as if we need to keep hustling and grinding away. Instead we are sitting there feeling depressed, anxious, and helpless. This is not the life I want for you. This is not the life I choose for myself.

When I made the announcement that I was going to be taking a leave of absence, the feedback I received was overwhelmingly positive. People said, "I am glad you are taking time to fill your cup." "You are so courageous." "I am jealous that you are taking this time." All overwhelming positives. And as for the critics, well, what I have learned is that first, people aren't really thinking about you as much as you think they are. Secondly, their reactions are a reflection of their own pains, regrets, and dreams. You'll go on your journey, and they will continue with theirs. The only people that truly matter is your inner circle—your immediate family.

So the next time you're feeling fear, get curious and reframe that fear.

- **Imposter syndrome:** Doubt is natural. What is it trying to tell me? And how do I use it to propel me forward?

- **Judgment:** I am proud of myself. No one else's perspective of me truly matters.

- **Fear of never getting back on the horse:** I like to create, so I am back on the horse, but it's a different one.

- **Fear of failure:** I have learned from failures and will continue to do so. Just begin again.

I've learned that doubt and fear are healthy. They motivate us to assess risks, develop contingency plans, and take preventive measures. Fear and doubt allow us to learn and grow. Fear keeps us alive! The difference is understanding what your fear is trying to tell you. Sometimes it is survival, and sometimes it is doubt. When you get that feeling in the pit of your stomach, ask, "What is this feeling trying to tell me? Is it trying to keep me alive or is it holding me back?" And then it's an evaluation process. You are not trapped. Use the signal fear is sending you. By embracing fear with curiosity, we can expand our boundaries, build resilience, and discover new capabilities within ourselves.

The Turning Point

Somewhere along the way, facing my fears seemed easier than the loneliness of feeling imprisoned and the endless urgent projects. The unknown suddenly seemed less scary than the pain of the known. I couldn't keep chugging along.

I knew I needed a change but felt like I should wait. What would I need to feel good about my decision? What logically did I need, and how would I emotionally prepare for this decision? All these questions promoted the need for reflection. However, the key question I asked myself was, "Do I see myself doing this for another year?"

Our family spent that Thanksgiving at the Gulf Shores, Alabama. I intentionally left my laptop at home and my phone off and in my luggage that week. For the first time in twenty years, I had a taste of freedom. After months of preparation, I knew it was time. I made the decision that week that I would resign on Monday when I returned from Thanksgiving.

I realized that I was completely fried. I felt that I wasn't contributing my best work and I wasn't growing from it. I dragged myself out of the box to breathe. When I talked to the CEO about leaving, I told her, "My heart just isn't in it anymore. It isn't fair to this company I helped grow. It's just time." Maybe I shouldn't have been so honest, but I didn't have anything to lose. I needed to be honest with myself.

What was the plan? An *intentional break*. I had no job lined up. I left a lot of money on the table. I just said, "I need to take the time for myself." It was such an odd feeling—an act of vulnerability and courage.

When I made that decision, I didn't know what it would bring or how I would feel. I just knew I needed to be free, whatever *free* meant. I knew I needed to get my mojo back and feel creative again. I was on a quest to find a way back to me and what was important to me.

When I talk about my career break to others, they often use the word *freedom*. I recall using that word too when I was in the box. Later I would realize that my choice was beyond a need for freedom.

It was autonomy and agency that I hungered for. I wanted to be authentic, have a voice, and do amazing work without the 141 other tasks clamoring for my attention. I wanted to focus on delivering the most impact.

Who Will Benefit?

So far, I've talked a lot about myself and my desires with this career break. I've shared my internal dialogue of barriers. You are so critically important. However, know that this break doesn't just benefit you. It benefits everyone around you!

My decision to take a career break was with the support of my spouse and my close circle. They saw and knew the toll it was taking on me. My wife especially saw the impact it was having—not just on me, but on our marriage and kids. I wasn't present, I was angry, and I was in reactive mode. And that reactive-mode person was not someone I was proud of.

What I've learned is that when I am better, when I take care of me, I am better for the people who matter most to me. And from that place, I can create more of a meaningful impact in the world. It's a positive cycle.

Free Diving

- What are the fears that are holding you back? What are they telling you?

- Write down the critics in your life and what they have said. Then let them go.

- What is your survival story? What has helped you get to this point in your life? Then reflect: Does it serve you now?

- Write down the people who will benefit from your career break. What does this mean for them?

 SCAN QR CODE FOR DOWNLOADABLE ACTIVITY
Visit www.careerbreakcompass.com

CHAPTER 5

A Passage Plan

"A goal without a plan is just a wish."

—Antoine de Saint-Exupéry

When my parents fled Vietnam after the north overtook the south, they needed a plan. My dad would often tell stories of the nights that led up to his family's escape. First, they needed to find a boat. Large ships were hard to come by and would make it obvious to the Viet Cong authorities they were fleeing. It was critical that they found the right boat that was also big enough to safely get forty-eight people to the Philippines.

Their next challenge was calculating how much fuel they needed to travel from Vietnam to the Philippines. My grandpa had made friends with a local police officer, whom he paid to access large plastic barrels that they would fill with gas. Gas was rationed to limit the ability for people to escape. So, one gallon at a time, my preteen dad and my grandpa would fill these forty-two-gallon barrels in the dead of night. It took patience, determination, and careful planning. If they were caught, they would be imprisoned and executed. This was a matter of life or death, but staying wasn't an option either.

Once the fuel was ready, the supplies needed to be gathered—enough food and water for their journey. As they pushed off the dock, paddling into the night as to not make a sound, they drifted into the dark sea. There they'd be cautious of other ships they'd find, fearful it was filled with pirates, who would raid their boats and kill everyone aboard. My parents' families were among the seven hundred thousand Vietnamese refugees who found a home in the United States. And this story has been a living narrative in my life.

Always be prepared. Always be ready to think on your feet. Always have a plan. Both my parents instilled this mindset of preparedness in me. My dad was a creative problem-solver, who would later become an electrical engineer. Growing up, if my brother or I had an idea to do something, my dad would ask us a series of questions. How are you going to make it happen? How much money will you need? How much time?

What happens if this obstacle gets in your way? I was trained at a young age to be ten steps ahead.

I love planning. I create one-, three-, five-, and ten-year plans every year to help me create a vision of where I'm going. At my first job, I had an incredible mentor who would ask all of us, "Where do you want to be in three years, in five years, and what skills can I help you gain to get there?" That's how I approached my career and my life. Where do I want to be, and what will it take?

Life happens, but I've always ascribed to Ben Franklin's quote, "By failing to prepare, you are preparing to fail." So of course planning a career break plan was critical!

All that to say, I needed to be ready. I needed a plan that was thought out and to be ready for any twists and turns. Then it would be time to fill those barrels.

What Type of Break?

When you're considering a break, there are several options beyond just quitting. Taking an extended leave from work can be a daunting task, but with the right approach, it is possible to negotiate a leave that works for both you and your employer. Whether you need time off for personal or family reasons, health issues, or simply to pursue other interests, careful planning and effective communication are key.

For some people, they may need a few weeks off to reset. For others, the break may need to be longer with a career transition afterward. There is no right or wrong answer. You have to decide what is right for you and your situation.

Remember in chapter 2, where we reviewed the different types of career breaks? Which one appealed most to you? Are you interested in exploring passion projects? Looking for more of an adventure? Just need time to recover and rest? Or are you looking for something more and need time to do some soul-searching? Whichever you decide, take the time to evaluate the type of time-off request that fits your needs.

There are a few ways people approach taking an extended break.

Types of Extended Time-Off Requests

○ **Vacation:** If you're planning a trip or need an extended break from work, you may request vacation time off. For example, you may have four weeks of vacation at your company. Perhaps you take off the time for a trip. Be sure to plan ahead and give your manager ample notice.

○ **Sabbatical:** A sabbatical is an extended leave where you typically return to your company. This can be paid or unpaid. There are numerous companies that now offer a paid sabbatical program for employees after a number of years of employment. Sabbaticals are also common for teachers or clergy members.

○ **Family or medical leave:** If you need time off to care for a family member or due to a personal medical issue, you may be eligible for family or medical leave. An eligible employee can take up to twelve workweeks of leave. Be sure to check with your company's policies for more details.

○ **Voluntary leave:** If the situations above don't meet your needs, you may want to explore a voluntary leave of absence. This could be a month- to three-month-long leave. Be sure to talk to your company's HR business partner on options.

○ **Resign:** You can make the decision to resign completely and use the time for a career break.

Note that mental health can qualify for short-term disability, depending on your situation. Be sure to connect with your company's HR department for more information.

How Long

Your decision about time depends on which path you choose. Research shows that it takes an average of 66 days for a new behavior to become automatic. It could be anywhere from 18 days to 254 days. I do recommend a minimum of two months, ideally three months off. Often, the first couple of weeks are spent acclimating to not logging into work and running errands. The real work starts three to four weeks into your time off. So you need to ensure that you allot enough time for each stage of the journey.

In this book, we walk through a ninety-day career break plan. This timeline helps you rebalance yourself, get clear on your priorities, practice them, and then reintegrate. However, 90 days may not be feasible for many people, so you can start with what works for you, then use the "bite-size breaks" activities throughout the next few chapters to help guide you.

How Much Money: Your Savings and Financial Plan

I will fully admit that my ability to take a career break is a privilege. My spouse carries our health insurance. I am middle to upper class. I've had well-paying jobs with good benefits my entire career. I had scholarships for college and graduate school, so I didn't have student debt. My parents taught me about finances, despite growing up in subsidized Section 8 housing. At a base level, I knew enough to make good decisions.

And when I didn't know an answer, I knew to ask for help. I started working with my financial advisor in 2016. That's six years ahead of my career break. We started to aggressively target savings in 2019. We set a savings target each month and invested monthly to prepare for retirement and to ensure that I could fund my career break.

It was a long game. I built this break into my five-year plan. It didn't happen on a whim. It wasn't rage quitting. It was patience and preparation.

So how did I plan my career break?

In reviewing expenses, I didn't take the bare minimum dollars we needed to cover our essentials. Instead, I planned to maintain our regular annual spending. This was for a couple of reasons. First, things happen, and I didn't want to drain my savings account on unplanned expenses. If you're not going back to your job, plan to find another role in time. Second, I knew we had become accustomed to a certain lifestyle and we would want to continue. We don't buy expensive furnishing or art. But we do enjoy dinners out, an annual vacation to the beach, our gym membership, and Starbucks runs.

How do you financially prepare for a career break? I suggest using what I call a BARE number, or Basic Amount to Recover and Energize.

1. **Review your spending**: How much have you spent on average in the last six months?

2. **Identify your situation**: Everyone's situation is different. Taking a sabbatical and then returning to your same workplace is different from taking a career break to shift to open your own business. Also, if you are taking longer than a year off, you'll need to plan for that accordingly.

   ○ Take your total six-month spending, including property tax, insurance costs, etc.

   ○ Then divide by 6, so that you have a real picture of your monthly spend.

   ○ Then factor up your spending by 20 percent (multiply by 1.2).

   ○ Then take the duration of your planned break and multiply by 1.5, to give yourself a buffer for a longer break.

○ Take your factored-up monthly spending multiplied by your factored-up timeline.

So let's say your average spending is $5,000 per month, and you plan to take a three-month break. You'd want to ensure that you have saved $27,000 ($5,000 × 1.2 = $6,000 × (3 × 1.5). If you are planning to take six months off, you'll need to save $54,000, and for a full year off, you'll want to save $108,600. If you are planning to travel or take trips during your break, be sure to add it to your BARE number.

Once you have that number, you're probably thinking, how am I going to get there?

○ **Understand your leave benefits:** If you are on a paid leave, the amount required to save is significantly less. Be sure to factor this into your estimate.

○ **Pay off debt:** This is going to be your first step. Eliminate as much high-interest debt, such as credit cards, as you can. Paying off debt enables you to save more aggressively.

○ **Save:** Saving is one of the most critical actions you can take. Cash in the bank gives you the freedom to take this career break, to change careers altogether, to retire early. I give credit to my financial advisor for continuously advising us to save. Either make more or save more. So we set savings targets each month.

○ **Manage your budget:** You can use your banking app, an Excel spreadsheet, or other budgeting app to help with this process. I use Copilot, which aggregates all my accounts and shows me daily and monthly spending. There is a small fee but the user interface is nice and easy to digest. Using this app, I can see how much I am spending in total each month. This will be helpful for when you are in your career break because you are living off of a fixed income.

- **Trim costs:** There may be ways for you to cut costs or trim the fat, as they say. Delay big purchases for thirty days, to see if you really need them. Are there subscriptions you don't use? Could you buy generics instead of name brands? Could you go see a movie on Tuesday cheap seats night instead of Friday?

- **Identify savings opportunities:** Over time, expenses start to increase, such as car and home insurance. When is the last time you got a competing quote? You can save hundreds.

- **Side gig:** Could you make additional income with side gigs? I took on side consulting projects. Even surveys, questionnaires, or interviews can make you some extra cash.

The next questions are about how to save and where to put the money. You can work with a financial advisor to identify ways to save. Here are a few popular options:

- **High-yield checking/savings account:** You may look at switching to a high-yield checking or savings account. It will be a small percentage but better than zero.

- **Brokerage account:** A brokerage account is an investment account that allows you to buy and sell investments such as stocks, bonds, mutual funds, and ETFs. You can go to a brokerage firm or even use robo-investing with platforms like Wealthfront or others.

- **CDs:** Certificate of deposit, or CDs, are time deposit accounts that pay you fixed interest over a fixed amount of time. For example, you can get a CD with a 5.1 percent APY with a one-year term. So let's say you put in $25,000. In a year, you'd earn $1,275 in interest.

The next questions are about how to address insurance, plan for your next venture, and build your emergency fund.

Insurance. Health insurance is extremely important as you consider your career break. If you're not resigning for a career break, you should continue to be covered by your company's insurance plan. However, if you make the decision to leave and need health insurance, there are a few options.

- **COBRA:** When you lose job-based insurance, you may be offered COBRA continuation coverage by your former employer.

- **Marketplace plans:** If you decline COBRA coverage or it is running out, you can enroll in a Marketplace plan. The federal government's Health Insurance Marketplace is a hub for comprehensive insurance. Also, each state features a health insurance exchange for its residents. Be sure to visit healthcare.gov for information about each state's exchanges.

Counsel dollars. For some of you, it may be important to bring in legal support. For executive roles with equity or specific contracts, you will want an attorney to review your documents. Be sure to plan for those expenses and the required time accordingly.

What's-next dollars. For some people who take career breaks, they intend to pivot from their current roles. For some, it's an industry change. For others, it's to pursue a passion elsewhere. For me, I wanted to open my own consulting practice. It had been a dream for years, and this pause would allow me to dedicate time and give myself a chance. That meant that I needed startup costs to be able to open my own business. My what's-next dollars were focused on ensuring that I had enough saved to be able to get me up and running.

Emergency fund. In the case of an emergency, be sure that you have at least three months' worth of living expenses, in addition to your career break fund. While you're on your career break, be sure to use your money wisely. Since you may not be making an income during this time, you'll need to think about living on a fixed budget if you weren't already.

Calculating the Impact of a Break on Retirement Savings

Many people are rightfully concerned with how a career break could impact their retirement savings. I know I was. For those who are taking an unpaid career break, you'll want to do some additional math.

First, how much would you contribute to your retirement savings over the months you will be on a break? Let's assume that those would grow at an annual 7 percent average rate of return. That would be your gap in savings. Let's take an example for a longer break. Let's say you're forty years old, typically contribute $18,500 a year to your 401(k), and are planning to take a one-year career gap next year. If you have $400,000 saved for retirement, your retirement fund without the break is $1.64 million. With your one-year career break, your retirement account is $1.6 million. So, the potential gap in your retirement savings with a one-year career break is $40,126.

As you review your full financial picture, don't forget to take this into account. There is a short-term financial impact, as well as a longer-term impact. However, $40,126 for one year off is not as significant an impact as you may have imagined.

When: Picking the Right Time

You need to reflect on when the seas are naturally calm or rough for you. The right time means different things to different people. There may be a financial incentive, such as an upcoming bonus payout. Or there may be life events, where taking time off aligns with your values and goals. For

MONEY BUYS FREEDOM

When I ask you what you want the most, your likely response is "to be happy." The challenge with *happy* in this definition is that it is a destination. The second challenge with *happy* is that it varies greatly from person to person. What's typically rooted in the desire for happiness is actually our desire for freedom. People want autonomy over their lives.

Angus Campbell, a psychologist at the University of Michigan, writes in his 1981 book, *The Sense of Well-Being in America*: "Having a strong sense of controlling one's life is a more dependable predictor of positive feelings of well-being than any of the objective conditions of life we have considered."

Reflect on the drivers to your burnout. Lack of control is likely very high on the list of causes. It was for me. I wanted autonomy and I wanted agency over my life and my work. At the root of it, I wanted the freedom to work on what I wanted, when I wanted, and with whom I wanted. It seemed simple but an ocean away. An aggressive savings and investment plan, a long-term picture of its impact, and the daily actions to balance joy and frugality were essential. That is why money matters in our preparation as well as our ongoing practices.

me, a new year was a natural time for me. Typically around my birthday, which is in January, I like to reflect on my year and set intentions for the upcoming year. So, January for me made sense to embark on this journey.

There are fresh-start days all throughout the year. It could be the start of spring or summer or perhaps when the kids go back to school. It could be Monday. Choosing the best time of the year depends on what you need, what you are looking for, and what you are going to do during your career break.

For example, if you live in a warmer climate, maybe the heat of the summer is a good time to go somewhere cooler to rest and recharge. Have kids, but need some solo time? Explore if you should start your career break when they will be in school, to give you time to focus on yourself. Or maybe you have a milestone coming up, like a child heading to college. Empty nesting can mean an opportunity to evaluate what you want next.

Think about a time when you can make a commitment to change—where you can put in the time, effort, and emotion to go through your transformation. It may sound cheesy, but that's what it is, a transformation. It's a shedding of what you've learned and been conditioned to believe.

How: Plan How You'll Use the Time

Your Itinerary at Sea

In my conversations about career breaks, those who have taken one without a plan often tell me, "I wish I had been more thoughtful about how I spent my time." They often spin because their schedule looks empty. And this emptiness somehow correlates to feelings of self-worth. A full calendar does not make you productive. A full calendar does not define your value, my friend.

However, I am wired like you, and an empty calendar made me feel panicked. So, the next stage is to identify how you will fill this calendar with intentional activities. I wanted to be thoughtful with how I would spend this precious time so that it didn't just pass by me. I needed this, and if I needed it, I needed to be sure I was going to be smart about it. I didn't want to sit on the couch binging Netflix and driving myself crazy for the next three months. I needed to know that how I was spending my days aligned with my goals.

It is important to create an *intentional* plan. Many of us type A personalities thrive off on structure and productivity. As humans we want to make progress. And just as you would create a plan to implement your annual goals, some structure is needed for your intentional time off. My belief is that you need some structure in a career break because it gives you permission to focus on recovery before you define what's next for work. It is common for us to react, to shift into action. And that action may mean spending your career break searching for jobs. That is not the intention of this time, which is why a plan of how the time is spent is critical.

I will share in later chapters that this also means scheduling time to sit and do nothing.

There's lots more on planning your time in the next section of the book.

Free Diving

- First, define the amount of time off you'd like to take. Is it a six-month or one-year break? Or are you planning to incorporate mini-breaks?

- Start working on your BARE number now. Get your Excel sheet out, identify how much you are currently spending, and plan how much you would need for two months, three months, or six months off.

- What type of break feels right to you? Will you come back to your company? Will you resign and find a new role or new path?

In the Resources section on page 225, you'll find a link to helpful templates.

SCAN QR CODE FOR DOWNLOADABLE ACTIVITY
Visit www.careerbreakcompass.com

CHAPTER 6

Time to Board

"Success does not lie in sticking to things. It lies in picking the right thing to stick to and quitting the rest."

—Annie Duke

After all this planning, it finally came time to hit the big green GO button. Or maybe more appropriately, it was a red STOP button. Time to get off this train.

I will be honest—I was never good at asking for what I wanted, let alone what I deserved. I never asked for a raise or a promotion. I never set boundaries at work. I answered the phone, emails, and texts, and I never hesitated to work late, come in early, or work weekends and holidays. I wasn't a martyr, I just did the work.

What I had gotten good at over the past few years was quitting. I would grit and grit and grit, until I couldn't stand it and then I'd quit. I was the queen of digging deep to get the job done, but I also knew when it was time to fold. Typically, I was good at reading the signs of an incoming change, so I'd leave after a tumultuous budget cycle, on the heels of an acquisition, or right before an entire shift in management. In my twenty years of working, I've had six jobs. My longest role was the one that I was in before I left, and it was for five years.

I guess you can say I was good at quitting when I needed to. However, it is never easy, and I was always a nervous wreck. I don't really know why, because they couldn't tell me "no." I guess it's the fear of letting someone down.

Even with all my practice in quitting, what I had never done was quit with no job lined up. Even when I quit my high school jobs at the mall or Hallmark Cards, there was always something else I was going to. This time, there was no other company or role. Somehow that did make it scarier to say out loud.

I guess it's like breaking up with someone. Somehow it makes sense when you say you found someone else. But if you say that you are leaving because you aren't happy, or you need more, or whatever—that seems more of a challenging conclusion to arrive at.

Since quitting can cause our stomach to flip, I thought it might be helpful to create a step-by-step guide for each situation, whether you are quitting, asking for a sabbatical, taking a leave of absence, or requesting leave under the Family and Medical Leave Act (FMLA).

How to Ask for a Sabbatical

When requesting a sabbatical from work, it's essential to approach the situation professionally and follow the appropriate steps. The first step is understanding if your company has a sabbatical program. If yes, here are some general steps to guide you:

1. **Review company policies.** Familiarize yourself with your company's policies and guidelines regarding sabbaticals. Check your employee handbook or consult with your human resources department to understand the specific requirements, eligibility criteria, and duration of sabbaticals allowed.

2. **Plan and prepare.** Determine the purpose and duration of your sabbatical. Develop a clear plan for how you intend to spend your time during the sabbatical and how it aligns with your personal and professional goals. Consider the benefits to both yourself and the company and outline them in your request.

3. **Research and propose a structure.** Investigate different sabbatical models and structures that could work for you and your employer. For instance, you might propose a full-time sabbatical for a specific period, a reduced work schedule, or a project-based sabbatical. Tailor the proposed structure to suit your needs and demonstrate how it could benefit both you and the organization.

4. **Schedule a meeting with your supervisor or manager.** Request a meeting with your immediate supervisor or manager to discuss your sabbatical request. It's crucial to

have a face-to-face conversation or a virtual meeting to present your proposal and provide any necessary context or explanation.

5. **Present your proposal.** During the meeting, clearly outline your reasons for requesting a sabbatical and explain how it aligns with your personal and professional growth. Share the benefits you anticipate, such as enhanced skills, renewed motivation, and fresh perspectives that you can bring back to your role after the sabbatical. Emphasize the value it can bring to the organization in the long term.

6. **Address potential concerns.** Anticipate any concerns your supervisor may have regarding your absence and be prepared to address them. Assure them that you have considered the impact on your workload and colleagues, propose solutions for coverage or delegation of responsibilities, and explain how you will ensure a smooth transition before and after the sabbatical.

7. **Formalize the agreement.** If your sabbatical request is approved, work with your supervisor and the appropriate HR personnel to formalize the agreement. Document the terms and conditions of the sabbatical, including the duration, start date, any salary adjustments or benefits during the sabbatical, and any expectations for reporting or communication during your absence.

8. **Plan for your absence.** Before your sabbatical begins, collaborate with your team and colleagues to ensure a seamless transition. Delegate tasks, provide necessary instructions or resources, and update any relevant stakeholders on your planned absence. Offer assistance in preparing documentation or transferring knowledge to mitigate any potential disruptions.

9. **Communicate during the sabbatical.** Stay in touch with your supervisor or designated contact person during

your sabbatical as agreed upon in the formal agreement. Maintain open lines of communication to address any unexpected issues, provide updates on your progress or learning experiences, and ensure a smooth reintegration when you return.

Remember, the specific steps may vary depending on your company's policies and procedures. It's crucial to follow your organization's guidelines, maintain open communication throughout the process, and ensure a clear understanding of expectations and arrangements related to your sabbatical.

How to Ask for a Medical or Caregiving Leave

When requesting medical or caregiving leave under the Family and Medical Leave Act, it's important to follow the specific steps outlined by your employer and comply with FMLA regulations. Common reasons for taking FMLA include the following:

- ○ Birth, adoption, or foster care placement of a child

- ○ Care for a spouse, child, or parent with health conditions

- ○ Self-care for the employee's own serious health condition, including mental health

Here are the general steps to guide you:

1. **Understand FMLA eligibility.** Familiarize yourself with the eligibility requirements of FMLA, including the number of hours worked, length of employment, and company size, as these factors can determine your eligibility for protected leave. Check with your human

resources department or refer to your employee handbook for specific information.

2. **Determine the need for leave.** Assess your situation and determine if your circumstances meet the criteria for FMLA-qualifying events. These can include your own serious health condition, caring for a family member with a serious health condition, childbirth and bonding with a newborn, or adoption/foster care placement.

3. **Notify your employer.** As soon as possible, inform your immediate supervisor or manager about your need for FMLA leave. Follow your company's specific protocol for requesting FMLA leave, which may involve filling out a formal request form or providing written notice.

4. **Provide necessary documentation.** Depending on the reason for your FMLA leave, you may need to provide medical certification or other supporting documentation. Consult your employer's FMLA policies to determine the specific requirements and obtain the necessary paperwork from your healthcare provider.

5. **Complete required forms.** Work with your employer to complete the appropriate FMLA paperwork, which typically includes the FMLA leave request form, medical certification form, and any other documentation your employer may require. Ensure that all forms are filled out accurately and submitted within the designated timeframe.

6. **Understand your rights and obligations.** Familiarize yourself with your rights and responsibilities under FMLA, such as the duration of leave allowed, job protection provisions, and any continued benefits during your leave. Be aware of any obligations you have, such as providing periodic updates on your status or returning to work after the designated leave period.

7. **Coordinate with your employer.** Communicate with your employer regarding the details of your leave, including the start and end dates, any intermittent or reduced schedule leave required, and any changes in your circumstances that may affect your leave period. Maintain open and ongoing communication throughout your FMLA leave.

8. **Prepare for your absence.** Before your leave begins, work with your supervisor and colleagues to create a plan for the coverage of your responsibilities during your absence. Provide necessary instructions, update project statuses, and make arrangements for a smooth transition of work. Ensure that all parties involved are aware of the procedures for contacting you during your leave, if necessary.

Remember, the FMLA process can vary based on your specific employer's policies and procedures. It's important to consult your human resources department or refer to your employee handbook for detailed information and guidance on requesting FMLA leave.

How to Ask for a Voluntary Leave of Absence

Remember that a voluntary leave of absence could be an option for you, and it is different from FMLA. A voluntary leave is typically a leave without pay, but where you would retain health insurance coverage. Companies may stipulate a minimum and maximum number of days off. For example, the leave may be a minimum of two weeks but up to twelve weeks.

Here are some general steps to help guide you:

1. **Review company policies.** Familiarize yourself with your company's policies regarding leaves of absence, including

the specific procedures, requirements, and any relevant documentation needed. This information is often outlined in your employee handbook or human resources materials.

2. **Determine the type and duration of leave.** Identify the type of leave you are seeking, such as medical leave, personal leave, or sabbatical, and decide on the duration of your absence. Be realistic and considerate of your work responsibilities and any impact your absence may have on colleagues or projects.

3. **Choose the right timing.** Consider the workload and upcoming projects in your department or team when selecting the appropriate time for your leave. Aim to request the absence at a time that minimizes disruption and allows for a smoother transition for your colleagues.

4. **Schedule a meeting with your supervisor or manager.** Request a meeting with your immediate supervisor or manager to discuss your leave of absence. It's essential to have a face-to-face conversation or a virtual meeting to communicate your request professionally and provide the necessary context.

5. **Prepare your request.** Prior to the meeting, prepare a written request that outlines the details of your leave. Include the specific dates or duration of your absence, the type of leave you are requesting, and a brief explanation for your request. Be concise, clear, and professional in your communication.

6. **Discuss your plans and responsibilities.** During the meeting, explain your reasons for the leave and emphasize the steps you will take to ensure a smooth transition in your absence. Offer suggestions for delegation of tasks or propose a plan to ensure minimal disruption to ongoing projects.

7. **Address potential concerns.** Anticipate any concerns your supervisor may have regarding your absence and be prepared to address them. Assure them of your commitment to your work, your willingness to assist with transition or training, and your intention to return to work fully prepared and engaged.

8. **Follow up with necessary documentation.** After obtaining approval for your leave, inquire about any documentation or forms that need to be completed. This may include a formal leave request form, medical certificates (if applicable), or any other supporting documentation required by your organization.

9. **Plan for your absence.** Before your leave begins, make arrangements for the smooth continuation of work in your absence. Communicate with colleagues or team members, provide necessary instructions or resources, and update any relevant stakeholders on your planned absence.

Remember, the specific steps may vary depending on your company's policies and procedures. It's essential to follow your organization's guidelines and maintain open communication throughout the process.

How to Quit

In the case where you intend to resign, below are a few steps to guide your communications and the transition process.

1. **Schedule a conversation with your boss.** It is important that the first conversation you have is with your direct manager. You do not need to wait until your next one-on-one. Just ask them if they have a few minutes.

2. **Start with the nice stuff.** I typically will thank them for the X years and everything that you have learned.

3. **Don't bury the headline.** After a sentence or two of appreciation, go into what you came there to say—you are leaving. Share your reasoning and that you are planning to take a career break.

4. **Provide a timeline.** You will need to decide how much lead time you'll give them. I've heard people tell their managers six months in advance to prepare for a career break or sabbatical. I think that is extremely generous. In my opinion a four- to six-week notice is sufficient. Here's why:

   a. The first one or two weeks is spent in denial (mostly on your manager's side). Also, you'll spend this time informing people, and their first week will be spent processing. The longer time you provide, the longer the denial phase will be.

   b. The next two weeks are spent preparing the team. Ensure that people know what they need to know. Schedule meetings with your direct reports twice a week.

   c. Then, if needed, the final two weeks allow you to be present to answer questions.

5. **Offer a transition plan.** During the meeting and in your resignation letter, express your willingness to assist with the transition process. Offer to document important processes, train a successor, or provide any other support that may be required to ensure a smooth handover of your responsibilities.

6. **Tie up loose ends.** As you approach your last working day, make sure to complete any pending tasks or projects, transfer knowledge to your colleagues, and ensure that important information or documents are properly organized and accessible to the relevant individuals. If you are a manager, try to write notes for your team for

their annual reviews or promotions. You've invested time into these individuals, so I try to leave them in a good spot.

7. **Exit interview and feedback.** If your company conducts exit interviews, take this opportunity to provide constructive feedback on your experience and share any insights or suggestions for improvement. Be honest, professional, and tactful in your feedback.

8. **Set your boundaries and be clear and consistent.** This is one I had not needed to do until my last role, and especially because I was leaving for a career break, not on to another job. For some reason, this concept of a career break makes people think your last day is more fluid. Once you state your end date, schedule your last meeting with your boss to walk through your transition notes. Say thank you and log off.

9. **Maintain professional relationships.** Throughout the process, maintain positive and professional relationships with your colleagues and supervisors. Connect with them on professional networking platforms and keep in touch, as these relationships can be valuable for future opportunities.

Stories from Career Breakers

Jordan: A month-long leave

Jordan is a VP of sales and marketing at a large organization. She had been at her company for the past seven years. Over that time, she navigated several downsizes and the resignations of her peers and her boss. Their team of fifteen people went down to three. She was responsible for her boss's role and her peer's sales role. She was exhausted, overworked, and extremely stressed. She felt personally responsible and invested in the company's success, yet it was out of her control. Jordan had a courageous conversation with her supervisor and she requested a month-long break—a paid leave of absence. It was approved. That act of bravery to communicate what she needed gave her one additional month of income and the time she needed to deeply evaluate her next move. In that time, Jordan and I worked together to help her reset, refresh, and define what type of role and company she wanted to work for next.

Gabriela: Ask for what you need

Gabriela is a manager at one of the largest and most prestigious global consulting firms. It's a place that is highly competitive to get into, and highly competitive to stay in. However, what makes this large organization unique is also its support for employee well-being and wellness. When I first connected with Gabriela, she was planning to resign to take a career break. As we explored her options, she did additional research and identified two other options. First, her company offered a sabbatical ranging from one to six months, as well as the option for short-term disability based on her mental health struggles. Gabriela worked with her HR department and manager to take a twelve-week short-term disability leave. Reviewing her company's options allowed her to choose what was the best fit for her situation. The key was to not let the fear of asking for what she needed hinder her time to rest and reset.

Morgan: A sabbatical path

Morgan knew she was going to take a paid sabbatical from work. There are organizations that offer paid sabbaticals as a benefit to their employees after years of service. In this process, she worked with her HR department to complete the necessary paperwork, transitioned her workload with a detailed transition plan, and set off on a six-week leave. She used the break to spend quality time with her family. She created a chaos-free system in the mornings that easily got the kids out the door for school and eased her into her day of personal projects.

My Story

As I shared, I am a decent quitter, but not someone who asks for what I need. In my mind, a sabbatical wasn't an option. I was wrong, and that helped broaden my point of view. When I resigned, our chief human resources officer called me and asked if I would be open to taking a leave of absence. As our CEO said, "What if we take a break, instead of breakup." (As a child of the nineties, all I could think of was Ross Geller saying, "We were on a break!") And that's what this was, a break, rather than a breakup.

I took a couple of months to decide what I wanted to do and to consider whether there was another role within the company that might be a good fit for me. They would backfill my role as I considered other opportunities. This was a genuinely kind offer, and one that I will forever appreciate. This process taught me a few important things: First, to be thankful to incredible leaders who recognize when employees need time to rest. Second, to research and be open to the options that exist for taking a career break. And finally, to ask for what you need. If you are on the fence about whether or not a career break or sabbatical is right for you, there is no harm in starting with asking for a sabbatical or a leave of absence.

Free Diving

- Decide which path you want to take. Then, draft the letter.

- Create your transition plan for work and for your career break. Who needs to know what? What will get deferred while you are on break? What will get delegated during this time?

- Be clear on how a career break will help you achieve your ultimate goals. Remember your North Star statement. What is your why?

CHAPTER 7

Sail Away, Sail Away

"You can't stop the waves, but you can learn to surf."

—Jon Kabat-Zinn

After all the communicating and transitioning, the time has finally come. Let the break commence!

Our brains like organization and rules. Before you embark on your voyage, you need to set some rules and guidelines to be sure that you maximize your time off.

Disconnect

Rule number one, disconnect from your device. In the era of connectedness, we are picking up our phones a hundred times a day as a result of random pings or aimless curiosity. This means that you need to set a dedicated time and space to disconnect.

Checklist to disconnect:

□ Delete unnecessary apps from your phone.

□ Set your phone on Do Not Disturb mode except for critical contacts (spouse, kids, etc.)

□ Remove your work equipment from your home office *or* don't go into your office.

□ Silence notifications from toxic contacts (or just block them).

□ Turn off all notifications.

□ Pick phone-free time blocks.

The best-case scenario is to spend the first two to three weeks of your break unplugged. Go somewhere that evokes awe for you. We'll talk more about this in our next chapter.

Set Boundaries from Emotional Pirates

As a people pleaser and over-functioner, I had a hard time setting boundaries. My "not good enough" voice meant that I was always available for work. In eighteen years, I never went on a vacation without my laptop, just in case there was an emergency. I would answer the phone whenever it rang. I would be at the mercy of every ping or notification.

I remember a time I was sick with the flu. I emailed my boss and said that I needed to take a sick day and would be unavailable.

They responded with, "I'm sorry to hear that. I need to connect with you on this project. Do you have time to chat?"

My response, "I am not feeling well and need to rest today."

Their response: "Okay, get some rest and I'll check in on you later."

Later happens: "Hey, do you have time to talk today?"

This was my fault. I didn't set the boundaries earlier in our relationship and would often be at my desk even if I had a fever and no voice.

What happens over time is a lot of built-up resentment. Nedra Glover Tawwab writes in her book *Set Boundaries Find Peace,* "Feeling taken advantage of, frustrated, irritated, annoyed, and bitter is the result of the resentment we feel when we don't set limits. Being resentful impacts the way we deal with people. It doesn't allow us to be our best selves in our relationships. It breeds conflict. It makes us paranoid. It puts up a wall."

I was a loyalty member on this resentment train, and I needed to get off. But that required some major changes. I needed time and space. So there I was, a little caterpillar, building my chrysalis or cocoon. At first, I was soft as I communicated my needs, but as I embarked on a journey to the true me, that shell got harder as my boundaries strengthened.

First, I needed a digital detox to start my career break, and that meant not talking to anyone except for my daughter and wife. Even those conversations would need to be minimal. I needed to be away from social media and the voices that liked to tell me what to do and how to do it. I needed space to hear myself. I turned off all notifications on my phone. I deleted apps that would disrupt me. I removed technology from my home office—no more computers: nada. Everything went into a box and into the basement.

Then, I picked a destination for three weeks where it would be pretty hard to find me, that would distract me, and had limited cell service. Some people have asked if a staycation could do the trick. I've found that it doesn't reset your brain enough. You can go to yoga and still come home to the basket of laundry and an endless to-do list. Staying home doesn't give you enough space to force you out of your routine.

Next, I needed to create a moat around me, so that I would choose who was allowed into my circle and keep others out. I committed to myself to take at least twelve weeks to reset, which meant I would limit my interactions with most of the world until I decided to reemerge. I am an introvert, so spending alone time sounded glorious. What I needed to let go of was feeling that I had to talk to my mom or best friend five times a week or even take those one-off calls from work to answer a quick question.

Your Crew: The Inner Circle

As you embark on your voyage, the people you keep close to you will play a critical role in your growth. This was something I learned through my own twelve-week process. I urge you to do this early. You will need to set a limited list of people whom you let into your mental, emotional, and physical space when you are on your break. I'm sure you can think of people who drain you. These are the people who bring drama, fill you with stress, or make you feel insecure.

The people you spend time with will shape your life and your future. Whom will you allow in? Jim Rohn says that we are the average of the five people we spend the most time with. I like that, so let's go with five, not including your children to whom you need to provide caregiving. These people will support you, and they won't be a critic or be jealous. You need people who are positive during this time.

- o The cheerleader

- o The mentor

- o The coach

- o The trusted friend

- o Your choice

I was extremely worried about sharing this journey with people, fearing their judgment. I'll tell you that most people don't understand it, because they cannot imagine a life where they aren't dragging themselves through each day. We are opting out of that. Unsubscribe me. So, when you talk about taking time off to reset and recharge, in theory they say, "Oh, how nice for you. I love that for you." However, when you're in it, they want to know what you are going to do next, immediately. But this is your time to breathe. Pick people to be in your inner circle who recognize the power of space and support you in it.

Remember this is your time to rest and reset. If you continue to do the same things you did before the break, nothing will change. You cannot change and grow without this step.

Having a hard time thinking of five? Don't worry, we have a community who can be your career break tribe. Go to the Resources section on page 225 for more information.

Stories from Career Breakers

Nicole's Social Network

Nicole created an intentional plan for her career break, with her deadline to kick off in midsummer. In her plan, she was thoughtful about what she would do, where she should go, and how she could facilitate an environment of growth. Nicole signed up to join a coworking space in her area that hosted professional development sessions and networking events. She made a plan to go to the gym every day, and she devoured information and ideas. What I love about Nicole's story is that she focused on people—and building a circle that would challenge her, teach her, and cheer her on. Nicole approached the career break as a sponge, and because of it she emerged more resilient and well connected so she could start her own business.

Brandon's Circle

Brandon was a director at a large organization, and he loved his job. As someone who focused on learning and development, he felt challenged and engaged in his work. Unfortunately, the corporate and bureaucratic environment got worse and he decided to walk away from his role. His decision to leave was rooted in a desire to reconnect with himself and his family. This was his inner circle, and during his break, he was very deliberate about how he spent his time. What he realized in his time off was that spending time with his loved ones, fully present and fully engaged, was worth it all. His gauge of success shifted from dollars to the freedom of time to spend with those in his circle.

The Career Break Road Map

After researching all the great work on burnout, I coupled it with my learnings around neuroplasticity—the ability of your brain to grow and learn—to create a plan that would reset and fully recharge.

There are four primary phases to this career break: play, pause, and plan, which happen during your break, and pursue, which commences after your break. I describe all of them in the following chapters, and they are based on a twelve-week break, though the timing of your break might differ a bit. Here's a snapshot of what we'll be digging into:

o **Play:** The first four weeks are focused on play. This is intended to shake the system and bring your focus to just having fun. I had read about the power of awe and wonder and to be childlike. I needed to feel free to just enjoy life. So play was important for me, and I'm certain it will be impactful for you. Play helps to invigorate your creative juices again, to feel in tune again with the things that once lit you up.

o **Pause:** The next four weeks are focused on pause. This is about grounding yourself in your purpose and focusing on listening to yourself and your desires. There is a significant body of research about the positive impact of meditation and mindfulness. Why not try it?

- **Plan:** The next four weeks are focused on planning. This is intended to help you integrate your learnings from the play and pause phases into your everyday life, and to redefine how you plan to work going forward.

- **Pursue:** The pursuit of your goals this time around is not only about professional achievements, it is also about ensuring a balanced and authentic life. Pursue is the integration of all of your learnings to create and maintain the life you design.

In the next parts of the book, we'll dive deep into each of these sections, the science behind them, and provide tools to help you incorporate the four *P*'s into your career break plan.

Create a Schedule

Research shows that having too little time leads to increased stress, but having an abundance of discretionary time can lower feelings of well-being, because of the low sense of productivity. Like most burnt-out people, you are likely a high-achieving productivity-focused person who lives by your schedule. You've probably lived your last couple of decades in back-to-back meetings. Suddenly the thought of an empty calendar is setting you into a panic.

A career break isn't just idle time. Yes, there should be space for that, but it should be intentional time. The days during my career break were full, but the difference was that I chose how I would spend them. I was intentional about how I spent my time to relax, recharge, be creative, and be purposeful.

As someone who spent a couple of decades in the corporate world, my brain works in PowerPoints and Excel spreadsheets. I visualize life as a pie chart. When we make an intention to free up space in the pie without a plan, another aspect of our life will just fill it in. So as you embark on your career break, it is natural to think that all the time you had previously spent on work will be just empty. But suddenly everything you wanted to catch up on over the last decade fills your schedule. Your twelve-hour workday gets filled with doctor's appointments, going to the gym, cleaning out the closet, working on that kitchen remodel. Unfortunately, you'll find that the pie doesn't just give you an open slice. No, it fills up.

There's no shortage of life things that you need to accomplish during this time. After all, you've been neglecting your closet full of clothes from high school, or the basement storage unit, or that home renovation project. However, go back to your North Star statement. Why are you taking this break? Does completing that task distract from that or add to that?

How do you make the time to be sure you're deeply rooted in *you*?

Using the play, pause, plan, and pursue framework, take the amount of time you intend to take and break each week or month into themes.

Then make a weekly schedule and start to allot how you would like to spend your time. Map out your ideal week as it aligns with your theme for your career break. The goal is to be sure that you are prioritizing how you will use your career break intentionally and actively.

Go to Resources on page 225 to access a link to the Break Plan, which you can use to map out your own break. Remember that this is meant to be a guide. If you wake up and need to know what to do, your schedule is there to help you. However, if you're in the middle of flow and enjoying yourself, stay with that feeling!

You are about to set off on a journey that will bring challenges. It will feel like a deep problem to solve. Lean into it.

Month	Theme
Month 1	Play
Month 2	Pause
Month 3	Plan
Month 4 and onward	Pursue

Where do you start when you have a problem? You look at the parts, you identify possibilities, and you test them. Life is just a long experiment.

Free Diving

- Who are the people who will be in your inner circle?

- Who are the people you will need to distance yourself from during this time period? What boundaries should you consider?

- Get clear and specific on how you will disconnect. What days, when, and where will you be?

- Review your ideal schedule for the duration of your break. You'll find a link to the templates in the Resources section (page 225).

Part 2

The Career Break:
Play, Pause, and Plan

CHAPTER 8

Power of Play

"We are never more fully alive, more completely
ourselves, or more deeply engrossed in
anything than when we are playing."

—Charles Schaefer

Have you ever watched a pod of dolphins jumping into the air? There's something beautiful and remarkable about watching these creatures somersault in the air and leap around boats. Each time they leap out of the water, they almost look as if they're smiling and laughing as they splash. Dolphins are incredibly curious and will play catch with a puffer fish or play hide-and-seek.

The highest level of brain development in animals happens during play. This is true for dolphins and it's true for humans. Play is essential for children's cognitive, physical, social, and emotional development. Through play, children learn about the world and themselves. They explore what they are capable of, build confidence and self-esteem, and develop resilience.

However, somewhere along the way adults forgot how to play. We got serious about achieving our goals and success and put fun and games aside. To top it off, studies show that there is a gender gap when it comes to play. A 2021 Bureau of Labor Statistics study states that men spend 5.6 hours per day pursuing leisure and sports activities, compared to 4.9 hours for women. And the age group with the least amount of leisure time? Those ages thirty-five to forty-four, with only 3.93 hours per day, compared to 5.7 hours for other age groups. That's 30 percent less leisure time a day.

My Story: How I Discovered I Needed Play

For you to better understand why play is important and why I needed to make play part of my career break, let me tell you about Amanda. Amanda was the first person I hired in the midst of the pandemic, which meant she was a remote hire (something that was to become the new normal). She was based in Virginia, so we didn't have the chance to interview in person, but I knew it was important for me to build the same rapport with her that I had with my onsite team. I believe that the best managers spend the time to get to know their employees. So that's what I focused on for Amanda's first ninety days—understanding what was important to her, how she worked, and who to connect her with in the organization to ensure her success.

Two months after Amanda started work she developed some health concerns and spent a few days in the hospital. She was always so worried about missing any work time, especially as a new employee. I was real with her—take care of yourself, the work will be here. The next week in our one-on-one, I asked her how she was doing and what I could do to support her. She looked very pale through our Zoom screen and she said, "I heard back from the doctors, and I need to tell you something. I found out that I have cancer." My heart dropped. She continued, "The doctors said they caught it early, and it's treatable. I will need some time off for treatments, but it won't impact my work. I can bring my laptop." I quickly replied, "Of course, take all the time you need, but you won't need to work during that time! Absolutely not." I didn't know the right words to say. "Thank you for telling me. The most important thing to me is that you take care of yourself. I care about you as a whole person. Don't worry about work. We'll figure it out."

As the months progressed, she would take mornings for treatments, but in that time, she only missed two meetings. She didn't want to tell the team about her diagnosis or treatment plan, so she just kept working. In our meetings, I'd see her kids in the background playing. I'd say, "If you're feeling good, go and take the kids out. Spend time with them. Work can wait."

When I think back to that conversation, I believe part of me needed to hear that too—that it was just work, and if necessary, work could wait. We are marketers; we're not saving lives. About a year later, the treatment and cancer started taking a toll on her, so she took some time off.

When the care package I sent her was returned by FedEx, I knew something wasn't right. Later that week, I got the call. Amanda's husband shared that she had passed. It was one of those calls that brings you to your knees.

Mortality is so real. Amanda was an incredible person. She was thoughtful, smart, always willing to jump in and help others, and with a somewhat dry sense of humor. I can still hear her voice in my head. Her loss was hard for me for a few reasons. I love my team, and losing someone I worked with every day was a grief I didn't expect. And on a personal note, I felt guilty. Should I have urged her more strongly to take time off sooner? Would she still be alive if she had taken care of herself better, if she wasn't working this entire time? Should I have shielded her more from the stress of our demanding expectations? If she wasn't stressed, would her immune system have been stronger, and would she still be alive today? Was it my fault?

Amanda's loss was relatable to me in several ways. We were about the same age, with kids the same age and a similar work ethic. Just ten years before Amanda's passing, my aunt passed away, leaving behind my two cousins. Both gone in a matter of months after diagnosis; both taken too soon.

I felt alone and scared. I had no one to turn to about missing Amanda, about seeing her name on my calendar for meetings she'd never join. There was no one who could comfort the guilt I felt for her stress and eroding health. I found the work of Elisabeth Kübler-Ross and David Kessler on grief. Kessler, author of *Finding Meaning: The Sixth Stage of Grief*, writes, "We tell ourselves things like, I feel sad, but I shouldn't feel that . . . Your work is to feel your sadness and fear and anger whether or not someone else is feeling something." And so I kept thinking to myself, "Why was Amanda so important to me, what values did she tap into that resonated with me, and more importantly, what could I do to honor her and her memory?" And that led me to ask myself the real underlying question, "What the hell am I doing with my life?"

Death changes everything. If you had fifteen months to live, how would that change your perspective? What would you do differently? There are three things that we can do with death. We can deny it. We can let it paralyze us. Or we can let it inspire us and be the catalyst for how we live. YOLO, the kids say. But my conflicting thoughts weren't about some fleeting need to experience bliss. I finally realized that I wasn't satisfied with my life and I needed to figure out how I wanted to live.

I had been in a grind for two decades. I was slogging my way through every single day. But work is work. Although you can do meaningful work, aren't the relationships and the impact you can have on the people you work with more important? And secondly—and this was really the root of it all for me—I wanted to value the time I had with my daughter, every single moment.

So, what does this heavy-hearted story have to do with play? I discovered that I needed to laugh and I needed to feel again. I needed to feel alive so that I could give that to my family, my daughter, and to the world. I knew that more play had to be part of my life.

How to Plan Play

"The creation of something new is not accomplished by the intellect but by the play instinct."
—Carl Jung

What comes up in your mind when you think about the word *play*? If you look up the word in the dictionary, it means to engage in activity for enjoyment and recreation rather than a serious or practical purpose. So, let's think about what play is and is not.

What is play?

   ○ It makes you feel good.

   ○ You feel free from time constraints. You're in flow.

   ○ You discover new things.

   ○ It allows you to be present.

   ○ You want it to last longer.

What is not play?

   ○ It doesn't serve a purpose.

   ○ It doesn't earn you money.

   ○ There's no obligation to do it.

   ○ It's not work.

In creating my career break plan, play needed to both revive and restore me. In my quest to get my mojo back, a major factor was to figure out how to get creative again. One of the key questions I set off to explore in this career break was how to change my mind. And changing my brain meant using play to integrate my left-brain regions, which are focused on logical, analytical, and emotional language, with my right-brain regions of creativity, expression, and sensations.

The issue with play is that it seems frivolous, a waste of time. We simply get in our own way. We come up with rationalizations as to why we aren't deserving. I've heard them all. Hell, I've said most of them myself. I believed play was a waste of time. I grew up in an immigrant household with a deeply instilled hard work ethic. If it wasn't productive, it was a waste of time. At the end of the day, we have lots of excuses for why we can't or won't engage in play, and here's just a few:

- Time constraints. "I don't have time!"

- Self-consciousness. "What if people judge me? It just feels silly."

- Negative beliefs. "What a waste of time. I need to be productive."

- Lack of inspiration. "I don't even know what I would do."

- Perfectionism. "If I'm not good at it, I'm not going to do it."

Our narrative around play has to shift. Play doesn't need to be earned; it doesn't need to be for the trophy. Sometimes, play is simply that. Put those excuses aside and instead focus on what types of play make sense for you.

In play therapy, clinical therapists actively work to help correct the "faulty wiring" that results from a trauma response and creates continued disruption in life. Play therapy creates new neural pathways to help damaged synapses recover and allow for healthy connections with the self and others, a better whole-brain function, increased resiliency, and overall increased well-being. If you want to reset and truly recover, you need to give yourself permission to play. It is not childish to be childlike. A sense of childlike wonder is likely what the doctor ordered to help you recharge. Let's dig into more on play.

Personalities for Play

Dr. Stuart Brown is the leading expert on play. He's the founder of the National Institute for Play and author of *Play: How It Shapes the Brain, Opens the Imagination, and Invigorates the Soul*. Dr. Brown identifies eight personalities of play:

1. **The Collector.** Collectors find joy in acquiring and organizing objects or experiences. These are folks who like to collect art, stamps, coins, pins, antiques, cars, shoes, etc. They get a thrill out of finding a unique piece, and they savor the experience of acquiring it.

2. **The Project Manager.** Project managers love planning and organizing activities for themselves and others. They enjoy taking charge of group activities, organizing events, or leading projects. These are the folks who are consumed with planning a wedding or their next vacation.

3. **The Narrator.** The narrator finds delight in creating and telling stories or engaging in imaginative play. They may enjoy writing stories, acting, or participating in role-playing games.

4. **The Athlete.** As you might imagine, the Athlete enjoys physical movement and sensory experiences. You'll find them engaging in dancing, yoga, sports, or any form of physical expression.

5. **The Explorer.** Explorers seek adventure and novelty. They enjoy discovering new places, trying new experiences, and engaging in activities that stimulate their curiosity.

6. **The Artist.** Artists find fulfillment in creative expression through various artistic mediums. They enjoy activities such as painting, drawing, sculpting, or playing a musical instrument.

7. **The Joker.** Jokers find joy in humor and playfulness. They enjoy telling jokes, engaging in lighthearted banter, and bringing laughter to themselves and others.

8. **The Competitor.** The competitor engages in play through competitive games with specific rules and enjoy the thrill of winning. The games can be solitary or social.

Reflect on the above personality types. Which one resonates the most with you?

Once you decide the type of play you want to engage in, there are a few other things to consider when you are planning play:

Who

- o Who will join you in Play? Will you include your partner, your family, a friend or two? Play doesn't need to be a solo experience. Think about who you'd like to join you.

- o Who do you need to contact to let them know you're going to be "off the grid"?

- o If you have family obligations, how do you ensure that you can take time away from them for your own fun and activity?

- o If you have small children who cannot be away from you, how can you identify childcare services to be sure you have some time off?

What

- o What are you going to do that sparks your fun?

- o What is your play personality and how can you brainstorm what you could do that aligns with your personality?

- o The goal is to disconnect from the things that are creating your burnout. What can you do to disconnect from your device and reconnect with your spark during play?

When

- Play is the first part of your journey, so when can you identify your start date?

- I recommend scheduling play for at least for a solid week. Can you make that happen? You deserve it.

Where

- If you need to stay local, what are areas that are a day's drive away that you can visit?

- Is there somewhere you love to go? Where in the world would you want to travel?

How

- How much do you need to save to make this happen?

- What planning and organizing needs to be implemented to be sure that you have this dedicated time to rest and reset?

Ideas for Play

Play doesn't require you to travel to another country. Although, if you want to head to Greece, I say do it! Play also doesn't require you to be the next Picasso. It only requires you to be curious and try something new and different. Put yourself in another setting, see the world differently. Do a puzzle. There are plenty of other options to explore. Here are a few suggestions:

- See the butterflies at the local botanical center or the zoo.

- Attend an immersive art experience—Van Gogh, Monet, anything.

- Shake your groove-thing at a music festival.

- Learn or practice a musical instrument.

- Try a new fun restaurant.

- Go to a trampoline park or play dodge ball.

- Laugh out loud at a comedy show.

- Immerse yourself in a puzzle or Legos. Your kids probably have some lying on the floor.

- Sign up for goat yoga. Yes, this is real, and it's real fun.

- Play pickleball.

- Visit an escape room.

Build Play into Your Schedule

During your career break, the goal is reigniting that spark inside you. Now that you have brainstormed all the things you can do around play, the next step is to create an action plan to do them. You don't need to do them all.

If you can, I highly recommend you plan a trip to play for at least one week, which will allow you to break out of your routine and put you in a new environment.

If that's not possible and you need to stay local, pick your top eight locally available activities around play. Then put them on the schedule to block off time for play. See Resources (page 225) for a link to a handy schedule. If you are taking four weeks off, schedule two play activities per week. This is your dedicated time to do whatever brings you joy.

Future dates: For the activities you don't have time to do, keep a list handy and go back to them post-break. The goal of practicing play is understanding how you can incorporate it into your everyday life—not just a career break.

Stories from Career Breakers

May's Time at the Ranch

May is an HR leader at high-growth organizations. She took a six-month career break to help her regain balance and take care of her physical and mental health. When I asked her what the most impactful experience in her career break was, May said it was spending time with family and animals. She worked with rescue and service dogs in training and spent time at a family ranch.

Mary's Ride to Freedom

Mary reached out to me two weeks into her career break. She had nothing lined up but was burned out and needed a fresh start. I asked her, "What is your plan for play?" Her plan: to spend it with her kids, doing what she had not prioritized before. She told me she went on a long bike ride with her ten-year-old and found it magical. It was something she couldn't do when she was working fifty-plus-hour weeks and completely stressed out.

Ava Finds Joy

Ava left her VP role with no job lined up, a similar story to mine. In one of our conversations, we had a chat about what play looked like in her career break. She shared that she spent some time organizing and decluttering (yes, that is considered fun for some people), but what was most impactful was a road trip with her mom, being able to walk her daughter to and from school, reading books and enjoying some Netflix shows. To use her word, it was "glorious." Before her break, Ava would find herself struggling to be present and play Legos with her kids. She would replay the day and then fast-forward to the long list of things she had to do. This career break gave her time to be present and enjoy her time with people she loved.

One of the greatest things I've learned about play is that it is interactive. Relationships with others is what helps bring aliveness. The connection with people we love, partaking in activities together, making memories—that's what play is all about.

My Story: What I Learned in Play

This may sound crazy to some of you, but my happy place is the happiest place on Earth—yep, you guessed it: Walt Disney World. I love Disney. There is something magical and awe-inspiring about being there. For me, it's a 4-D experience—the sight, smells, sounds, textures, all of it!

So, what did I do during play? I went to Disney World of course! To kick off my break, it was important to me to reconnect with my family, and that meant my family, including my parents, spent a week at Disney World. We went to Magic Kingdom for New Year's Eve and watched the glorious fireworks above Cinderella's castle. We rode the classic rides and the new ones. I screamed at the top of my lungs on the new *Guardians of the Galaxy* ride with my dad and my wife. We watched the giraffes and hippos at Animal Kingdom. And we ate our fill of popcorn from our iridescent Mickey popcorn bucket. It really was magical.

After that, I needed to find an activity that would help me disconnect from my devices and most people. My daughter was three years old at the time, and though it was important to me to spend time with her, I also needed a childcare option so I could also focus just on me.

Similar to the theme of this book, I decided that the rest of play would entail a two-week back-to-back cruise that would enable me to shut off my phone, continue to have fun, and play and be ever-present with my family, while also exploring places I had never been. My daughter and I boarded the cruise ship, and we island-hopped through the Caribbean.

It was an incredibly fun experience, and it was also the beginning of the self-exploration I needed.

First, let me explain that I had never been on a cruise ship before. I typically like schedules, but I was trying on a new me, a more relaxed me that wasn't as structured, so I tried not to plan too much. Play needs to have a spontaneous nature, right? So I shouldn't follow the obligations of a schedule. But, what I found myself doing on the first few nights of the cruise was *everything*. I didn't want to miss a thing. We ran up and down the ship for the scavenger hunt, joined activities in random rooms, and attended all the character meet-and-greets. My daughter and I were exhausted and I was frustrated. I consciously made the decision to stop. We decided to let go of FOMO and just do what we wanted to do when we felt like it. Even if that was just hanging out in our room and watching movies. That was lesson number one: do what you want, without fear of missing out.

On our cruise, there were assigned dinner times. When dinner would roll around, I'd rush my daughter to the dining room. My three-year-old was not accustomed to long sit-down dinners without the assistance of a phone. We'd finish our appetizers and she was ready to go. For the first three nights, I'd try to bribe—I mean incentivize—her with a toy. "We can go to the store and buy you something to play with, if you just go to dinner." It was exhausting negotiating and arguing with my toddler, so on the third night, we skipped our sit-down dinner and opted for room service. The next morning, our waiter said, "Oh, I was waiting for you! We missed you last night."

And there it was, the guilt. I didn't want to let our waiter down. WHAT?! What was wrong with me? Who cared? He was going to get paid and tipped regardless of whether or not I showed up at dinner. I was on the cruise for me! This isn't supposed to be stressful or obligatory. Play should make you feel good, not have time constraints, and create a feeling that you want it to keep lasting. The rushing around was not bringing me joy and it wasn't play.

———

That's when I realized that my people pleasing was out of control and that I was putting a stranger's feelings (and I don't really think he cared anyway, to be honest) above my own. Then and there I stopped worrying. Lesson number two: focus on you, and let go of the people pleaser.

Once I gave myself permission to go with the flow, my daughter and I were both more at ease. We all feed off each other's energy, and she was calmer because I was calmer. By the second week we were full of laughter. We played hard, and then we took naps. (Before, I secretly frowned upon napping, because rest was for the weak. Not anymore!) During my career break, I gave myself permission to rest and we just took care of ourselves.

Lesson number three: do not strive for perfection. Some people say that you should do something that makes you feel afraid. Well, here I was on a boat in the middle of an ocean completely separated from my work life. Often, I didn't know what to do with my idle time, and as a lifelong pacer, I was getting fifteen thousand steps a day. I will not lie to you and say that I was comfortable and it was always glorious.

That first week on the ship I would drop off Ellis at the kids' club and find myself aimlessly walking around. I had no idea what to do on my own. When we stopped at our first port in San Juan, Puerto Rico, I was scared to leave the ship. I was consumed with anxiety at the thought of taking my three-year-old somewhere I wasn't familiar with. We stayed on the ship that day.

This is where the beauty of scheduling an extended time away for play kicks in. Instead of beating myself up over my fear, I just tried again. We went to Tortola in the British Virgin Islands and spent the day on the beach. Whenever we do something for the first time, it is scary as hell. Once I gave myself permission to feel that fear and not listen to my inner critic, trying again was easier.

Don't strive for perfection on this journey. That is not the point. The point is having compassion for others and yourself. The next time, feel the courage inside you pull you toward exploration.

As I reflected on my weeks of play during my career break, what I realized most was that I stopped controlling everything and instead shifted my mindset. If I had tried creating purpose to the play, forced us to go to everything, or worried about what other people thought of me, I wouldn't have enjoyed myself in the slightest. I needed to let go and enjoy the moments, and that's exactly what we did.

———————

Play is critical for children as much as it is for adults. Over time, we lose play and joke, "Oh, to be young again." The truth is, it is a choice we can make. Play allows us to explore, understand our environments, and problem-solve at any age. It connects us to others and ourselves. It gets us up and moving, which makes us happier and healthier. Studies in the fields of psychology, education, and neuroscience have all supported the importance of play. So, step one to well-being is ensuring you incorporate play into your life more frequently.

Free Diving

- In the first column of the table that follows, make a list of things you want to do for your play dates. They can be big or small, while traveling or at home.

- In the second column, rank them based on what is accessible to you and doable during your break.

- In the third column, include how much it will cost for each play date activity.

Idea	Rank	Cost $	Play Date

- Using the template accessible via the Resources section (page 225), schedule at least five activities around play during your break. Even if you are traveling for three weeks of play, you need to have two activities you will do at home that are budget-friendly.

- Choosing a mini-break? Schedule one play date a week from the list.

- The key to joy is to let go. What did you let go of to maximize play?

BITE-SIZE BREAK IDEAS

Having fun doesn't always require a lot of money or weeks off of work. Here's a list of short and cheap ways people can have fun:

1. Outdoor picnic: Pack a homemade meal, snacks, and drinks and head to a local park for a picnic with friends or family.

2. Board games or card games: Gather friends or family for a game night with classic board games or card games you already own.

3. Cooking or baking: Experiment with new recipes, bake cookies, or prepare a meal from scratch using ingredients at home.

4. Go for a bike ride or hike: Go for a long bike ride with family or friends. Getting out and doing a physically challenging activity can help you recharge.

5. Visit a museum or gallery: Look for free or discounted admission days to explore art, history, and culture.

6. Explore your city: Be a tourist in your own town by discovering new neighborhoods, parks, and attractions.

Remember, the key to having fun on a budget and without extended time off is to be open to trying new activities and finding joy in simple pleasures.

CHAPTER 9

Power to Pause

"If the ocean can calm itself, so can you.
We are both salt water mixed with air."

—*Nayyirah Waheed*

When you envision a peaceful setting, it's likely you imagine something related to water. A still lake in the morning, the gentle sound of the ocean waves on the sand, a stream rolling over a bed of rocks. Water is fluid, adaptable, and tranquil. It cleanses, heals, and brings peace. As you shift to the next part of your journey into the pause phase, water will continue to play a role in your rejuvenation.

Pause was the most transformative portion of my journey. Deep down, I knew this would be the hardest and most rewarding work for me. Play was intended to shake out the cobwebs. But pause was the intentional act of clearing my mind and trusting my gut. In this chapter, I'll share various ideas on how you can integrate pause into your break. For many, this is the most challenging part of the journey, and it is also the most critical.

How to Prepare for Your Pause

The intention of pause is to ensure that you are allowing the time and space to listen to the voice that's already inside you. In all the research I've done on recovering from burnout, there is a lot of discussion around mindfulness and meditation.

Research shows that meditation reduces stress, helps manage anxiety, promotes self-awareness, and improves self-image and mental health. For these reasons, I think some form of meditation needs to be part of your pause phase.

Here's the science of why.

Reset Your Nervous System

Let's start with understanding the nervous system.

A complex network of nerves and cells that transmit signals between different parts of the body, the nervous system plays a crucial role in controlling our thoughts, movements, sensations, and vital organ functions. One key component of the nervous system is the autonomic nervous system (ANS), which is responsible for moderating our body's response to external and internal stressors.

The ANS is made up of two branches: the sympathetic nervous system (SNS) and the parasympathetic nervous system (PNS). SNS is our fight-or-flight response. It increases our heart rate, dilates our pupils, and releases stress hormones like adrenaline and cortisol. PNS is our rest-and-digest response. It promotes relaxation and restoration. The PNS slows down our heart rate, constricts our pupils, and promotes digestion and healing. It allows our body to rest, repair, and recover.

If you are struggling with chronic stress or prolonged stress (a.k.a. burnout), then you have an overactive SNS and an underactive PNS. What does that mean? Well, you live in a state with elevated blood pressure and heightened anxiety, while having difficulty with digestion, sleep, and relaxation. Basically, your nervous system is dysregulated.

The signs of a dysregulated nervous system and burnout are pretty closely aligned. They look like these:

o Persistent anxiety or excessive worry

o Feelings of restlessness or irritability

o Difficulty sleeping or insomnia

o Digestive issues, such as stomach pain or bloating

o Chronic fatigue or low energy levels

o Muscle tension or headaches

o Increased sensitivity to sensory stimuli

o Impaired concentration or memory problems

o Mood swings or emotional instability

○ Weakened immune system and increased suscepti-
bility to illness

The challenge with a dysregulated nervous system is that it
doesn't just go away on its own. Similar to burnout, rest and
a vacation aren't going to miraculously solve it.

How Do You Reset the Nervous System?

To do this I thought I needed a Mr. Miyagi, a sensei who
could guide me through the journey. Turns out, resetting just
requires basic stuff that we all deprioritize. I call it a pause.
And once you implement practices that reset the nervous
system, you'll find that they help burnout as well.

These include the following:

Mindfulness and Meditation: By intentionally directing our
attention to the sensations of the body, thoughts, and
emotions, we can reduce stress and enhance our ability to
respond rather than react to challenging situations.

○ Download a meditation app and give it a try.

○ Schedule your meditation. Try for first thing in the
morning.

○ Write in a journal.

Physical Movement and Exercise Exercise releases endor-
phins, which are natural mood-boosting chemicals that
alleviate stress and anxiety.

○ Schedule thirty to forty-five minutes of moderate
exercise each day.

○ Schedule a walk through a garden or go for a hike.

Adequate Sleep and Rest: Rest is the foundation of mental health. It is so critical to prioritize restful sleep. During sleep, our body repairs tissues, consolidates memories, and balances neurotransmitters.

○ Aim for seven to nine hours of sleep each night.

○ Plan your bedtime. Set a routine to unwind and disconnect from devices.

○ Try a nighttime meditation to help you settle in and prepare for sleep.

○ Give yourself permission to take a nap.

○ For those who experience insomnia, this may be a challenge. Be patient with yourself.

Nutrition and Hydration: Eating well and drinking lots of water are essential for nourishing the nervous system. Aim for a balanced diet rich in whole foods, including fruits, vegetables, lean proteins, and healthy fats. Stay hydrated.

○ Plan and cook your meals to eat whole healthy foods.

○ Get a gallon-size water bottle and keep it with you all day.

○ Limit caffeine and alcohol. I am a caffeine addict, so this one is tough for me. A reminder that helps me is that caffeine doesn't give me energy, it just numbs the signals telling my brain I am tired.

Therapeutic Bodywork. This can be massage, acupuncture, and chiropractic care and can be beneficial for resetting the nervous system. These practices help release muscle tension, improve circulation, and promote relaxation.

o Schedule a message.

o Use a massage device at home.

Relaxing Activities: Find hobbies or practices that bring you joy. These activities help shift your focus away from stressors and activate the pleasure centers in the brain.

o Find a fun book to read.

o Get out in your garden.

o Nap in a hammock.

o Play an instrument.

Supportive Relationships: Surround yourself with individuals who uplift and support you. Engage in meaningful conversations, seek emotional support when needed, and prioritize quality time with loved ones.

o Reconnect with people who share your similar journey. You're not alone in this.

o Check out different interest groups. Interested in journaling? Check out an *Artist's Way* group. Interested in meditation? Go to a local meditation center to meet others who share similar interests.

o Join the Career Break community (find us in the Resources section on page 225).

All the above can be done inexpensively and in your own home or close by. If your time and budget allow, plan a retreat to a wellness center that has these activities. There are numerous retreat centers that provide you the space to meditate, practice breathwork, exercise, sleep, and so on. This fully immersive experience allows you to be completely dedicated to this practice without distractions. They also allow you to meet others who are on similar journeys of self-care.

———

As you review the list, it's important to make these regular, habitual exercises. Be sure to block time on your calendar for a pause break daily. I often suggest a morning and midday pause break. Set a recurring meeting on your calendar for fifteen minutes every morning and in the afternoon to take a moment to pause. Prefer a paper calendar? Or an alarm reminder? Whatever you do, do what works best for you, as long as you are regularly engaging in pause.

In the Resource section (page 225), I have included a calendar template to help you identify ideal times for pause, as well as other tools to support you.

Challenges That Arise in Pause

In my interviews and coaching work, pause is the most interesting part of the journey for many in the beginning, but admittedly, it's the hardest to get through. It often will take longer than you think, and it will take a lot out of you. A client once reflected to me, "Pause kicked my ass. It took everything out of me, exhausted me, and yet filled me with a newness that I needed to heal." Pause is grounded in the belief that we can heal and transform. And in order to do that, we need to slow down and be present.

Typically, a few topics will arise while you are in pause that you should look out for:

1. **Your desire to act will fool you.** While you are in your quiet space, that inner critic in your head will emerge and tell you that you need to *do* something: you need to act; you need to apply for a hundred jobs. It will tell you your worth is defined by what you *do*. All the programming you have been conditioned to believe will

come screaming at you. Don't let it fool you. This is your sea monster. We'll talk more about that in a future chapter. Recognize it. Acknowledge it. But do not feel compelled to act because of it. Your time to pause is just as important as "doing" something.

2. **Commitment is required.** Pause requires commitment. Your burnout will not go away on its own. Play is fun and sometimes distracting, which is what it's intended to be. Pause switches gears and points your periscope inward. Go back to your North Star. Remember why you are here and why are you taking this break.

Pause will probably make you feel uncomfortable, likely because you haven't spent a lot of time here in your life. If I'm honest, when I was in pause I was sometimes kicking and screaming as I tried to get through it. This practice requires vulnerability and openness. For many of us, our compartmentalizing walls have allowed us to survive. It's important to take down these walls and explore why we created them in the first place. You didn't choose to take a career break to maintain the status quo, so don't give up now. Stay committed.

3. **Loneliness is real.** The journey will sometimes feel lonely. Your desire to go on this voyage is not one that everyone can follow or even understand. Your friends, family, and other loose ties may be on different paths. The loneliness will feel real but know that you aren't alone. Use pause as an opportunity to find new connections. There are many people who are on a similar voyage. Find in-person and online communities to stay connected and motivated along your way (see Resources on page 225).

My Story: What I Learned in Pause

I chose the month of February for my pause. I knew that coming off four weeks of galivanting around was going to require some reintegration. The goal of my career break was to fully reset my mind, but what I didn't know was that it wasn't about my mind at all. Instead, I needed to get more in tune with my body, heart, and spirit. The truth was that I needed to get out of my head to do that.

Meditation Retreat: Profound Change for a Nonbeliever

When I started my career break research, I knew I wanted to do something focused on mindfulness. I talked to my friend Nicole who is an avid meditator and told her I could barely get through five minutes of meditating. She recommended a place called CIVANA, which became my beginner's guide for this journey.

For my first week of pause, I packed my bags, got on a plane, and headed to Arizona. I landed late at night and drove the one hour from Phoenix to Carefree (yup, that's a real town!) in the pitch black of night. The next morning, I looked at my itinerary, grabbed my water bottle, and headed to my first class: Breathwork for Beginners.

As I stepped outside, I felt the chill air, an odd feeling that didn't align with my expectations of Arizona. But I went with it. My head was still fuzzy, just the standard glaze that had been there for the past few years, also potentially as a result of dehydration. Drink more water, I told myself. Or, better yet, where's the coffee?

This first class helped set the stage for the remainder of the week. Breathwork. And I am a chronic clencher—I grind my teeth and hold my breath, and I did this all subconsciously. I'd be sitting in a meeting and my heart would race, and I'd realize I was holding my breath. In class, we learned a few breathing techniques, but most importantly, our instructor taught us how to *pay attention to* the breath. "What is your breath telling you?" she asked. "When you inhale, where is there resistance? Do you have challenges receiving? When you exhale, do you experience pauses? Where are you struggling to let go of?" All I could think was, "Are you effing kidding me, lady? You don't know me." But I could feel my inhales come in, and then I could feel the hold in my lungs and the resistance to release. It was true. I couldn't let go.

The awareness of the breath changed my mindset as I moved through the remainder of my week. I took the meditation and mindfulness track during my time there. Classes included daily meditation, nightly sound healing meditations, journaling meditation, and conscious breathing.

The most profound class for me was conscious breathwork. Sound healing and the other meditation classes were cleansing, but conscious breathing left me feeling free. I wanted more. What I learned later was that conscious breathing was breathwork that would lead to altered states of consciousness. We were guided in a ninety-minute meditation where we'd breathe rapidly in and out for a few minutes and then breathe normally. In a room with loud music to drown out the noise of other participants' experiences, we lay down with our eyes covered to help with relaxation. Our instructor guided us when to breathe and when to deepen our relaxation. Surrender, she'd say. Go deeper. Go deeper.

After a few minutes, we'd breathe normally. For the next few minutes, I was floating, just soaring through the air. At one point I was holding some fruit in my hand. I tried to wiggle my fingers, but I couldn't, I was in another plane. I felt light and free but still connected to my body, the room, and the others in it. I could hear the sound of someone crying to my left side. Our instructor had said that this experience was a release, and people's reactions could be crying, laughter, and even bliss.

After that experience, I needed to understand more. It was curiosity but also a longing to feel as free as I did for those moments. It was not like me to go into an experience unprepared and unknowledgeable. But there I was. So of course the natural thing would be to research everything.

What the Hell Is Breathwork?

I've never been a big believer in crystals, astrology, or any other woo-woo spirituality. So, when I returned from my week in Arizona, I needed to understand the science. What did I learn?

Experts state that the average resting adult breathes about 12 to 20 times per minute. That's 28,800 breaths a day. For most, these breaths are unconscious. Conscious breathwork is the awareness of how the breath moves in and out of the body. Conscious breathing work is rooted in allowing CO_2 to build up in the blood. This then enhances the cardio-inhibitory response of the vagus nerve when you exhale and stimulates your parasympathetic system, which results in a calm and relaxed feeling. Yogic breathing or pranayama yoga was the first doctrine to build a theory around respiratory control. In Sanskrit, *prana* means "vital life force," and *yama* means "to gain control."

There are many different types of conscious breathing practices. Some are more common than others.

- o Diaphragmatic breathing starts with putting one hand on your chest and a hand on your stomach. Breathe in through your nose until you can't take in any more air, expanding your stomach. Then purse your lips and slowly exhale for four seconds and feel your stomach contract.

- o Box breathing, also known as square breathing, is a technique where you inhale for four seconds, hold for four seconds, exhale for four seconds, then hold for four seconds. Then repeat. It's used by Navy SEALs, athletes, and nurses.

○ Anulom Vilom, or alternate nostril breathing, involves holding one nostril closed while inhaling, then holding the other nostril closed while exhaling. This is reversed then repeated. It is said to create an immediately calming effect.

○ Wim Hof breathing was named after Dutch extreme athlete Wim Hof, commonly known as the Iceman. The Wim Hof Method starts with taking in a strong inhale through the nose and letting out a relaxed exhale from the mouth. Repeat for thirty breaths. On the thirtieth breath, exhale to 90 percent and hold for as long as you can. When you feel your body needs a breath, inhale fully and hold for fifteen seconds before releasing. The Wim Hof Method fully engages the diaphragm.

○ Holotropic Breathwork is a therapeutic breathing practice that produces an altered state of consciousness. The process involves breathing at a fast rate for minutes or hours. This then changes the balance of CO_2 and oxygen in your body. You're awake but the default receptors in your brain are not, which allows you to unlock something different within you. These breathing techniques have their warnings—it's a no-go if you're pregnant or have a heart condition.

Holotropic Breathwork is the type of conscious breathwork I explored. There have been various studies on the impact of Holotropic breathwork sessions. A 2013 study with more than eleven thousand people over a twelve-year period suggested that Holotropic breathwork could treat a range of psychological life issues with no adverse reactions (Eyerman,

24–27). Those who participated in the study reported emotional catharsis. As I am writing this, researchers at Johns Hopkins University are conducting a study to use breathwork to help with anxiety, depression, trauma, or PTSD symptoms.

So wait, conscious breathing, the simple act of paying attention to my breath, could help reduce anxiety and depression? I was all in. Depending on what you need and how much time you have, there is a conscious breathwork technique that can work for you.

Meditation for Beginners

Before my career break, everything I read about reducing the risk of burnout said to meditate. My friends told me to give it a try, and all my attempts were short-lived. I couldn't make it a habit primarily because I didn't see the benefit.

I'm not sure why I rejected meditation. After all, it ran in my family. It's estimated that nearly 60 percent of the population in Vietnam are Buddhist. My mother's side of the family is Buddhist, and my uncles had spent time in a Buddhist monastery in Vietnam. When my uncle would come visit us, he'd sit and meditate several times a day. I remember running around the house and seeing my uncle, calmly sitting in front of a window. I didn't get it at the time. I do now.

When I was in college, I had a ritual. Every Friday, my friends knew not to bother me after my last class. I would joke that I needed to be horizontal from the overwhelm of the week. I would schedule this time, and if you were looking for me, I would be lying on the floor in my dorm room, staring at the ceiling in silence. Lying there, I could feel the grooves of the carpet under my hand, and my breath would start to slow into longer inhales and exhales. This was my time and space to just be—without expectations. This was my safe space. Once I had this hour, I'd roll over, slowly stand up, and be ready to go. I now have language for this—I was meditating.

Periodically over the next couple of decades, I would, again, find myself horizontal on the floor, staring at the ceiling. It was always there when I needed it. Yet, somewhere along the way, I forgot that safe space. It was likely that a house full of people, kids, and the endless to-do list simply took up space, and my me-time disappeared.

The time I spent in pause was the reminder I so deeply craved. Our meditations at the retreat weren't sitting, but lying down. And there, on the yoga mat, I could feel the threads of the blanket just as I used to feel the grooves of the carpet. As the overhead lights started to dim, I was reminded of my college dorm ceiling. I felt safe again.

I went from not lasting even five minutes to meditating for four hours a day. My mind and my body craved meditating. So, if a "can't sit still" pacer like me can do it, so can you. Unfortunately, I don't have time to meditate for four hours a day in the real world. So, I figured out ways to integrate it into my life in a meaningful and realistic way.

Ways to Regularly Practice Meditation

The new mindset and practices that I learned (or relearned) during my four weeks of pause were practices that needed to continue throughout the break—and into my life once the career break ended. Pause is a daily muscle to flex. Here are a few practices I incorporated into my life and that I still do today:

○ **Schedule the time:** Make this a priority. I know we are all incredibly busy, but if you schedule your meditation time, you can make it happen. Every morning, I allot ten to fifteen minutes to meditation after I drop off my daughter at school. For some people, waking up at 5:00 a.m. works for them. Not me. I typically meditate around 8:30 or 9:00 a.m.

If I miss it, I make sure to get in a midday meditation. Do what works for you.

○ **Choose the right position for you**: Everyone has a different meditation position. Personally, I prefer to lie down. I like to feel my whole body melting into the floor. This helps me be more present. Sometimes I'm not in a place where I can do that, so if I am sitting for a meditation, I just like to have my back supported.

○ **Meditate anywhere**: If I'm not home and it's my time to meditate, I will find anywhere to meditate. I head to a parking lot, put my car in park, push my seat back, and close my eyes. Although I prefer lying down, sometimes it's just not possible, but that doesn't mean I give up this meditation time. I make sure meditation is inserted into my day.

○ **Drown out the noise**: Sometimes I listen to a guided meditation through *Ten Percent Happier* or Peloton. Sometimes I'll put on the meditation playlist I found on Spotify. Other times, I just pop in my noise-canceling headphones and listen to my breath. There is no right way to do it, just the way that works for you when you need it.

○ **Breathwork**: There are a ton of different breathing techniques. There's box breathing, calming breathing techniques, breathing with pursed lips, diaphragmatic breathing, breathing through alternate nostrils, and so on. Pick what works for you. For me, counting in my head is too distracting and doesn't help me relax, so I don't do that. I just go with the feeling in my body. I visualize the breath coming in and filling my chest, then feel it exhale out of my body all the way. No counting, just feeling.

○ **Yoga nidra**: Often referred to as "yogic sleep," yoga nidra is a state of conscious relaxation and meditation that guides you into a deep, relaxed state while remaining awake and aware. When I heard that thirty minutes of practicing yoga nidra equates to two to four hours of restful sleep, I had to try this, and it was glorious. It is a systematic method of inducing complete physical, mental, and emotional relaxation. The goal is to achieve a state of profound relaxation and heightened awareness, facilitating inner healing and self-discovery.

○ **Find a group session.** There are meditation teachers who host in-person sessions weekly or online group sessions for six, eight, or more weeks. Having someone else guide your experience can be extremely helpful and gives a sense of community.

I am continuing to learn about myself along this journey. Meditating is still very new to me, but I know that I physically and mentally feel different after it. There is an openness in the stillness of meditation that allows us to listen and sometimes receive the message we need to hear. That is why I continue this practice.

Meditation is like shaking a snow globe. First, the defined patterns of the day and my routine get flipped upside down. As the snow slowly falls, it's almost as if time is suspended. Each flake is positioned differently than before. Each shake is a fresh start, a different perspective.

Journaling: Getting Real with How I Feel

"The quieter you become, the more you are able to hear."
—Rumi

I have been a journaler all my life. I still recall my Pocahontas lock-and-key journal. I found Julia Cameron's *The Artist's Way* through a mentor in 2007 and thus began my practice of morning pages. I'd wake up and write, just write three pages of whatever came to mind. No critique, just words on pages. This practice would come and go throughout the next fifteen years. But as with meditation in college, I lost the journaling habit. Once again, life got in the way.

When I made the decision to take a career break, I knew I wanted to start up that practice again. I needed to get a brand-new journal, my favorite pen, and back to my morning pages. At the meditation retreat, I took a course on transformative journaling. Our presenter brought up *The Artist's Way* as a tool to help clear the mind, and for me, it was an affirmation to be intentional and deliberate with journaling this time.

As with the meditation skills that I acquired, the journaling practice I revived during the pause phase continued through the remainder of my career break and now into my daily life.

What I have learned in doing morning pages is that when I try to avoid that practice, I am actually avoiding myself. Morning pages give me the clarity to start my day, and it almost serves as an unintentional intention-setting exercise for where I am and how I want to show up that day. Typically, what I am trying to bury arises in my morning pages. And once they are out of my head and onto the paper, somehow those thoughts shift to something tangible and it makes the challenge I am working through easier to manage.

As you are writing your pages, you will notice that a tone of judgment might peek through from time to time. Your inner critic will rear its ugly head and try to undermine you. Mine often asks me why I've done something a certain way, or it will rerun events to prove why I was wrong or dumb or worthless. When that happens, I just write the letter *S* and circle it. This is the Shitty Censor. Acknowledge it but then move on. Don't let it continue to take up more space on your three pages. Just add the *S*, circle it, and move on. You'll be surprised at how effective that is.

Whether you are a beginner or avid journaler, know that there's no wrong way to write. The goal is to get the mental chatter and clutter out of your brain and onto a piece of paper. You don't need to revisit it; you don't need to take an action. You just need to clear your mind.

Choosing Joy

Through meditation and journaling, what I was truly learning during the pause weeks was the choice of joy. As I write this, I am in a six-week breathwork course and our theme for this week is "I have a right to my joy." This rings so strongly and truthfully for me. For so many of us, we have delayed gratification for so long that we don't even know how to embrace joy when it's in front of us. We are so used to punishing ourselves for that great vacation because the return to work on Monday is going to feel soul crushing. Or worse, we plan this incredible vacation and one small thing goes awry and then we feel the entire vacation is a waste of time. We expect that life should be a certain way, that people should act a certain way, and the things we cannot control will always land just perfectly. That simply is not real life.

"If you want to understand stress, begin by realizing that you carry around with you your own set of preconceived notions of how things should be. It is based upon these emotions that you assert your will to resist what has already happened," wrote Michael A. Singer in *The Untethered Soul.*

In pause, I made a very intentional decision to choose joy. To me, choosing joy was about observing life and following the pull that would come from it. Don't get me wrong, this is an incredible struggle. If you are like me, your high-achieving anxiety has fueled you to always be prepared like the best Boy Scout that ever lived. You thrived off being ten steps ahead and wore that badge proudly.

Choosing joy will require you to let go. Joy is about letting go of expectations and being in a moment you cannot control.

Years ago, a coach once asked me, "What is your reaction to the word *surrender*?" It was like my throat closed up. I was filled with fear and horror, and those were just my first reactions. A warmth started to rise inside me. Not the warm, fuzzy, comforting-blanket kind of warmth. It was the heat of panic, then anger. My body was reacting as if it were being attacked by a bear. Needless to say, my reaction to surrender was poor.

Almost exactly ten years after this conversation, I found myself in my career break. It took me a decade to realize that I was resisting and pushing through to continue achieving. I spent so much energy and time in resistance, it became toxic for me. *Surrender* continues to be a word I struggle with, but less and less each day. It serves as a signal to me to let go and realize I can't control everything.

I am confident that pause will have a meaningful impact for you, as it has for my clients and for me personally. Give yourself the permission to be present, to let go of expectation, and to enjoy the pause.

Forms of Rest

The intention to pause is the act of giving yourself permission to rest. That rest could be meditation, as I've previously shared, but there are numerous other types of rest. In Dr. Saundra Dalton-Smith's book *Sacred Rest*, she outlines seven types of rest: physical, mental, emotional, sensory, creative, social, and spiritual. You can focus on the type of rest and self-care you truly need.

1. **Physical rest:** Physical rest is giving your body time to recover and repair itself. We often think of this as taking a nap, getting a message, or stretching.

2. **Mental rest:** Mental rest is giving our mind a rest. This is the act of giving our brains time to recharge so that we can be better focused and productive. This may include meditation, setting your phone to Do Not Disturb mode, or limiting apps.

3. **Emotional rest:** Emotional rest allows us time and space to process our feelings. This could include spending time alone, journaling, or spending time in nature.

4. **Sensory rest:** Sensory rest gives us a reprieve from the noise, lights, and other stimulus around us. This could include turning off the TV and spending time in a quiet space, practicing deep breathing, or listening to calming music.

5. **Creative rest:** Creative rest gives our brain time to explore new ideas and enables it to problem-solve, be inspired, and be motivated. This could include taking a break from work, finding a hobby, or enjoying a creative activity such as cooking, drawing, or painting.

6. **Social rest:** Social rest gives us time to recharge and maintain emotional boundaries. Socializing, especially for introverts, can be draining, and social rest helps us maintain connections with others by spending time alone.

7. **Spiritual rest:** Spiritual rest allows us to connect to our inner selves. This could include meditating, practicing yoga, or spending time in nature.

As you go through your career break and beyond it, engage in different forms of rest or pause to ensure you are recharging. No one is going to give you permission to do this work except for you. Give yourself the space to be present and intentional about how you reset. Remember, this work will take trial and error. Some days may be better and easier than others. Lean into the experimentation of it. Find what works for you and your life. As I've shared, meditation, breathwork, and journaling are all practices I have found work for me. Yours may be very different. Take the time and space to explore and allow yourself to fully experience it.

Stories from Career Breakers

Avery's Journey to Peace

So much of what we talk about during pause is really about prioritizing peace. When Avery set off on her career break, two themes included peace and pause. High achievers love high-paced, high-stakes environments. Unfortunately, our nervous systems are not big fans. To reset, Avery needed to retrain herself to practice patience, both for herself and others. The act of slowing down was key to reprogramming her inclination to sprint. She gave herself permission to heal. Her first step was making peace with her decision to walk away from her high-paying, high-visibility job. Doing this gave her permission to heal and focus on her time in her career break. Next, she managed her sleep. She would often find herself having nightmares about work. Allowing herself to rest and slow down was critical.

What I love about Avery's story is that pause is an inside-out job. It reiterates the need to give ourselves permission to be in our break. It also starts to shed the programming of achievement and success that we have latched on to.

Free Diving

- In the first column of the table that follows, make a list of things you want to do for your pause dates. They can be big or small, while traveling or at home.

- In the second column, rank them based on what is accessible to you and doable during your break.

- In the third column, include how much it will cost for each pause date activity.

Idea	Rank	Cost $	Pause Date

- Using the template accessible via the Resources section (page 225), schedule daily pause activities. They should include the following:

    (1) mediation or mindfulness for at least ten minutes a day

    (2) a gratitude practice—use a journal and write one thing you're thankful for daily

- Pick a time of day and duration where you will lock up your phone. Free time from your phone will force you to be present.

 SCAN QR CODE FOR DOWNLOADABLE ACTIVITY
Visit www.careerbreakcompass.com

BITE-SIZE BREAKS

Don't have the time or money to go to a meditation retreat? Check out these resources that helped me.

- Sharon Salzberg: Salzberg is a meditation teacher and offers a fantastic beginner's course. I also love her loving kindness meditations.

- Ten Happier App: A great series of guided meditations.

- Meditation centers: They are all over the place and probably near you. Some yoga studios offer meditation.

- Other apps: Calm, Headspace, Insight Timer, Balance.

- Float tanks: These are sensory deprivation tanks, where people submerge in a tank filled with water and Epsom salt.

- Nature bathing: Just go sit in nature. Find a pond, take a walk, go sit by the beach. The ability to be present in nature is so powerful.

CHAPTER 10

Wrestling with Your Sea Monster

"The heart of man is very much like the sea,
it has its storms, it has its tides
and in its depths it has its pearls too."

—*Vincent van Gogh*

As a high achiever and people pleaser, I always had this voice inside me telling me that I wasn't good enough. This voice could be a motivator or it could be debilitating. It propelled me to prove it wrong, but on bad days, it would leave me feeling alone and self-criticizing. One of the fears I had in starting meditation was spending time with that voice.

We all have a bit of that inner critic. For some it is louder than others. For all of you, it took a lot of courage to get to the point where you recognized your need to take a break. When you're at sea and the sky is black and you have no idea what direction you are headed, the panic sets in and your sea monsters emerge.

My Story: How I Wrestle My Monster

As I mentioned earlier, meditation has not always been easy for me. I'm actually pretty terrible at it at the beginning of every session. My first few minutes are often me trying to remember not to fight myself. My breath becomes rapid, my brain starts to go into hyper-plan mode, and all I want to do is get up and be productive. I almost have to fight to keep my eyelids from springing open, to the point where they are twitching. It takes everything in me to stay put.

But if I continue to push through, I start to feel heavier. My breath starts to slow. I can hear my breath and feel my chest and belly expand. My eyelids relax, and things go dark. This is the first moment when I feel I'm finally me. The voices will come in and out, my planning obsession will start to float. The difference is that in this state, I can see them float in their own bubbles and I just let them fly away. There's no controlling, there's just being with them. This is how I wrestle with my monster.

Meditation has allowed me to accept all the bubbles and currents in my life. The ones that bump into each other, the ones that float, the cold ones, and the warm ones.

My two greatest takeaways as an amateur meditator are (1) you can always begin again, and (2) always try to be gentler and kinder to yourself.

The first is a good reminder that shit is always going to happen. You're going to get distracted. And the list of things you need to do in the "real" world will shove themselves into your brain. It's fine. It's there. You can begin again. And so I take a breath slowly, feel it fill me, and exhale. I don't need to do anything with them. I don't have to fix myself, beat myself up about screwing up meditation, correct my thoughts, or put out any fires. I can accept myself. As I am.

For the second, practicing self-compassion and loving kindness meditation has helped me change how I treat myself. Unlike self-esteem, which relies on external validation, self-compassion is rooted in self-acceptance and understanding.

I was introduced to different self-compassion practices during my pause journey as part of the inner work I needed to do. I have a panel of inner critics in my head constantly judging my decisions, thoughts, and actions. I have been in a lifelong struggle with them. What I didn't know was what to do about my panel of critics. Through these practices, I've taken away my self-critics' megaphone, which makes it easier to ignore them.

Self-compassion practices can be divided into three components: self-kindness, common humanity, and mindfulness.

- Self-kindness involves treating oneself with kindness rather than with self-criticism or judgment.

- Common humanity is recognizing that every person feels inadequate or makes mistakes at times and understanding that this is an inherent part of being human.

- Mindfulness involves acknowledging difficult emotions without judgment so that one can make conscious decisions about how to respond to them.

Ultimately, self-compassionate practices are about learning to balance both kindness toward ourselves and accountability for our actions in order to create lasting positive change in our lives. Research shows that consistent engagement in self-compassionate practices produces measurable long-term improvements in overall well-being, making it well worth the effort for anyone who wishes to create lasting positive change for themselves.

There are a variety of self-compassion practices including guided journaling, loving kindness meditation, using mantras, or practicing positive self-talk. Try a few out in the Free Diving exercises.

Stories from Career Breakers

For those I've interviewed and those I've worked with in my coaching practice, this feeling is extremely common. It's important to get a handle on it, or it will debilitate you for the remainder of your break.

My client Dean deeply struggled with his inner critic. Prior to leaving his role as a VP in an extremely prominent company, he was always on—nights, weekends, holidays. Work was his identity, but it was making him miserable. So he left his job, but he had no plan. After a couple of weeks turned into a couple of months without another job, the panic set in. Dean's challenge was that he had not wrestled with his monster to get clear on what it was he really needed and wanted. As time went on, that voice in his head got louder and louder. The voice he needed to hear was the soft, comforting voice telling him that he was on the right path and that he just needed to allow himself to be there. Together we worked on using self-compassion exercises to rebuild his confidence so that he could hear his positive inner voice and gain clarity on what he wanted in his life and in his work.

Dean is not alone. I've talked with those who have shared similar stories and who have questioned if they made the right decision. They were frozen by fear rather than allowing themselves to experience freedom. Freedom is what we long for, and when we finally have it, sometimes we don't know what to do with it and feel guilty for even taking the step to find it.

Each decision we make is one to learn from. If you've been beating yourself up most of your life, ask yourself this: What if you approached it differently? What if you gave yourself permission to be where you are, right now? What if you said, I'm here to battle my sea monster instead of running away from it?

Free Diving

- Practice loving kindness meditation (see Resources, page 225)

- Make a list of your five greatest strengths. Don't know what they are? Ask a friend or loved one.

- Identify how you will handle your own sea monster when it emerges. What are the three to five techniques you'll use?

- Do you have an inner gremlin or inner critic? Write it a letter. Tell it how it can be more effective in supporting your goals and efforts. Let the critic shift to be helpful rather than hurtful.

- Select a few mantras that will help you be resilient during your career break. They may include "I am enough." "I deserve love and kindness." "I am doing my best."

BITE-SIZE BREAKS

Try one of these resources to help you practice self-compassion. Links can be found in the Resources section (page 225).

- Kristin Neff is a professor at University of Texas and is known as the pioneer of self-compassion work. She provides exercises and guided meditations on her website.

- Sharon Salzberg is a *New York Times* bestselling author and Buddhist meditation teacher. She developed guided meditations on Loving Kindness.

- Check out a few meditation apps such as Ten Percent Happier or Calm.

CHAPTER 11

Plan to Empower

"Passion is a fickle magnet: it pulls you toward your
current interests. Values are a steady compass: they
point you toward a future purpose. Passion brings
immediate joy. Values provide lasting meaning."

—Adam Grant

So, you've taken the time to play and you've mindfully paused, but to make this career break truly effective, you need a plan that will take you beyond the break and back into the kind of everyday life that will energize and support you. The plan phase is focused on how you want to reintegrate, and how you'll incorporate the aspects of your play and pause phases into your ongoing life.

"Prior planning promises pleasant passages" goes the saying. When you're in this vast, complex ocean, you will need to spend time deciding where to go next for smoother passages. Similarly, you'll need to balance what you want to do after your time off that allows you to be fulfilled throughout your life.

How to Plan

Figuring out the person you want to be, what you want to do with your life, and how you want to live feels like a massive undertaking. That is why planning is so critical. It gives you a framework that reduces the overwhelm and maximizes its impact.

In this chapter, I outline the steps to help you ensure alignment with your core values and create a work/life balance that supports those core values.

Let's dig into each one of these.

Core Values Exercise

Step 1. Who you are starts with what is important to you. From the list of core values on the next two pages (also available as a downloadable exercise accessible in the Resources section, page 225), circle or write down every word that resonates with you. Don't overthink it, just write and circle.

Abundance	Equality	Knowledge
Accountability	Ethics	Leadership
Achievement	Excellence	Learning
Adaptability	Fairness	Legacy
Adventure	Faith	Leisure
Altruism	Family	Love
Ambition	Financial stability	Loyalty
Authenticity	Forgiveness	Making an impact
Autonomy	Freedom	Nature
Balance	Friendship	Openness
Beauty	Fun	Optimism
Bravery	Future generations	Order
Belonging	Generosity	Parenting
Career	Giving back	Patience
Caring	Grace	Patriotism
Change	Gratitude	Peace
Collaboration	Growth	Perseverance
Commitment	Harmony	Personal
Community	Health	fulfillment
Compassion	Home	Power
Competence	Honesty	Pride
Competition	Hope	Prosperity
Confidence	Humility	Recognition
Connection	Humor	Reliability
Contentment	Inclusion	Resourcefulness
Contribution	Independence	Respect
Cooperation	Influence	Responsibility
Courage	Initiative	Risk-taking
Creativity	Integrity	Safety
Curiosity	Intuition	Security
Dignity	Job security	Self-discipline
Diversity	Joy	Self-expression
Environment	Justice	Self-respect
Efficiency	Kindness	Serenity

Service	Thrift	Usefulness
Simplicity	Time	Vision
Spirituality	Tradition	Vulnerability
Sportsmanship	Travel	Wealth
Stewardship	Trust	Well-being
Success	Truth	Wholeheartedness
Sustainability	Understanding	Wisdom
Teamwork	Uniqueness	

Step 2. Once you have your set of words, review them again. Be sure you understand what they mean. Do a quick search for definitions. You may find other keywords that resonate better with you. Write those down.

Step 3: Once you have a list of words that resonate with you, the next step is to group them into similar themes. How are these words related? Group them in a way that makes sense to you. Create a maximum of five groups. I try to target three or four.

Step 4: Based on the list of groupings, select one word per column that best resonates with you! This word should be representative of the entire column. For example, *Growth* represents my words for curiosity and learning. Circle it. Don't overthink it; there is no right or wrong answer.

Step 5: The circled words from each column are your core values. Describe each core value starting with a verb, as I've done below.

- **Growth:** to seek opportunities for curiosity and learning

- **Authenticity:** to live openly and expand a sense of community and inclusion

- **Balance:** to act in ways that promote well-being and balance in my life

Examples:

Group 1	Group 2	Group 3	Group 4	Group 5
Achievement	(Authenticity)	(Balance)	Caring	Truth
Ambition	Belonging	Simplicity	Family	Fairness
Career	Community	Collaboration	Future generations	Freedom
Financial stability	Diversity	Gratitude	Connection	Fun
(Growth)	Safety	Health	(Love)	Honesty
Success	Equality	Travel	Parenting	(Integrity)
Competence	Harmony	Well-being	Making a difference	Courage
Contribution	Inclusion			Joy
Wealth	Openness			Leisure
Creativity				Personal fulfillment
Curiosity				Vulnerability

o **Love:** to care and connect with the people in my life

o **Integrity:** to live and act with honesty, standing up against injustices

Step 6: Test them. As you look at your core values, how do they make you feel? Do they align with who you are? Do they feel truly personal to you? Do they elicit an emotional response?

Remember, you are a work in progress. Nothing is final. Reflect on them, come back to them, rewrite them.

Identify Your Strengths

Acknowledge how far you've come! Your history can help inform your future. Let's start by reflecting on memorable experiences you've had in your lifetime. What are some life and career successes you've experienced? Make a list of the unique strengths and talents that you drew upon. Think about the following:

o What are you naturally good at? (e.g., problem-solving, communication, leadership)

o What skills have you honed through education or work experience?

Can't think of what you're good at? Call a loved one or friend and ask them, "What would you say are my top three strengths?"

Craft Your North Star Statement

Using the insights gained from Core Values and Strengths exercise, reflect on the North Star vision statement you drafted on page 49. Does it still align with your core values? Revise your North Star statement if needed.

Here are a few examples:

- Oprah Winfrey (media mogul and philanthropist): "To be a teacher. And to be known for inspiring my students to be more than they thought they could be."

- Nelson Mandela (Anti-apartheid revolutionary and South African president): "I have cherished the ideal of a democratic and free society in which all persons live together in harmony and with equal opportunities. It is an ideal which I hope to live for and to achieve. But if needs be, it is an ideal for which I am prepared to die."

- Malala Yousafzai (education activist and Nobel laureate): "To empower girls through education and create a world where every girl can learn and lead without fear."

- Warren Buffett (investor and philanthropist): "To allocate my time, energy, and resources to things I believe will significantly improve the lives of others."

- Me: "To empower and inspire individuals to embrace their whole, authentic selves, fostering a community built on equity, diversity, and mutual respect, where every person can thrive and contribute their gifts to the world."

Create a Plan to Live Your Values

The Core Values and Strengths exercises will tell you what is important to you. The next step is to turn those desires and values into action. But how?

Our daily choices are a reflection of how important our values and desires are to us. That doesn't mean that you have to quit your job, but it might. It doesn't mean that you have to spend the next two hundred days on a cruise ship exploring the world because you wrote down *travel*, but it might. It is dependent on you and what the most important things are to you.

Your core values and desires do not need to be in conflict with your life and your work. In fact, they put into perspective your work, your life, and how you live it.

Think about your values as objectives and key results initiatives (OKRIs). When we look at business goals, we often talk about OKRIs because they are used by organizations as part of goal setting. How are you applying this practice to your daily life? We're going to do it now.

Take a look at your core values. Then use the OKRI framework to fill in your key results and the initiatives that will support them coming to fruition.

Follow this framework: I will [objective] as measured by [key results] by doing [initiatives]. This framework helps you continue to live in alignment with your core values.

Your mission statement is your North Star. It guides your OKRIs.

Once you have crafted your initial draft, let it sit and settle. It is a work in progress. You can share your mission statement with trusted friends and family members for feedback. Others may offer valuable insights or suggestions to help improve your mission statement. Adjust as needed until it feels right. Remember that your mission statement may evolve over time and based on the season, or circumstances, of your life. Be open to revising it as needed.

Sample:

North Star	To empower and inspire individuals to embrace their whole, authentic selves, fostering a community built on equity, diversity, and mutual respect, where every person can thrive and contribute their gifts to the world.		
Rank	**Objective**	**Key Results**	**Initiatives**
1	Growth: Seek opportunities for curiosity and learning	Read at least 20 books/year Interview 100 people/year	• Read 2 books/month • Create interview framework of questions and interview 10 people per month
2	Balance: Act in ways that promote well-being and balance in my life and others'	Focus on daily habits of meditation and mindfulness Support coaching clients in developing balance	• Practice conscious breathing every morning • Create a framework to support clients in balance, and pilot with 15 people
3	Love and Belonging: Care for and connect with the people in my life	Be more present with my family and friends In my work interactions, focus on demonstrating care and support and create a sense of belonging	• Schedule weekly connects with my spouse • Plan a weekly date night with my kiddo • Practice active inquiry and listening in all meetings
4	Authenticity: Live openly and expand a sense of community and inclusion	Show up as my true self and not worry about people pleasing Focus on work that aligns with my values and desires; set boundaries when it doesn't	• Build a decision tree to help me ensure values alignment • Create my decline-message templates to make it easier to set boundaries and say no
5	Integrity: Live and act with honesty, standing against injustices	To share my honest perspective on the negative impact of toxic work cultures To promote diversity, equality, and inclusion (DEI) efforts through my work and in my community	• Start posting daily on LinkedIn about my experience and create a community • Volunteer at my daughter's school for all DEI efforts and support candidates who align with my beliefs

Free Diving

- Write a letter to yourself as though it is twenty years in the future. What would Future You tell Present You, as you are planning your career break? Share what you learned about your career break and how the time positively impacted your life.

- Complete the Core Values exercise.

- Next, review your strengths.

- Using both your core values and strengths, craft your North Star Mission Statement.

- Next, create a Plan that aligns with your core values and North Star Statement. This is how you can live your values going forward.

BITE-SIZE BREAKS

Interested in digging more into you? Are you a fan of personality tests? In my opinion, personality tests are flawed, but they are helpful tools for dialogue and introspection. Personality tests give us language to talk about ourselves and consider some truths within us.

Online Assessments (Free and Paid)

You can access these online personality assessments online. Check out the Resources section (page 225) for details.

- Sparketype Assessment can be used by individuals or organizations. It helps you discover what energizes and inspires you and whether your current work supports your Sparketype. Leaders can also use sparketypes to help increase motivation, performance, and personal growth.

- VIA Character Strengths is a psychometrically validated personality test that measures an individual's strengths. Discovering your strengths can help you better overcome challenges and feel more fulfilled professionally and personally.

- CliftonStrengths, formerly known as Strengths-Finder, is a psychometric instrument developed by the Gallup Institute. The assessment measures unique talents, or what they define as natural patterns of thinking, feeling, and behaving.

- Myers-Briggs Type Indicator (MBTI) is a popular self-reported questionnaire that identifies a person's personality type, strengths, and preferences.

- Enneagram is a system of personality typing that describes how people see the world and how they manage their emotions.

Once you've completed these assessments, journal using a few of these prompts:

- What are the similarities from these assessments?

- What are five to eight keywords that resonated with you as you read through the assessments?

- When you review those keywords, write down how they made you feel.

CHAPTER 12

Spyglass: Career Exploration

*"Without leaps of imagination or dreaming,
we lose the excitement of possibilities.
Dreaming, after all, is a form of planning."*

—Gloria Steinem

When was the last time you intentionally explored what you wanted in your career and how it fit into your life? For many of us, we have gone from one defined path to another. Grade school, high school, college, maybe grad school, job. Then you follow the career progression outlined by HR or a department leader and climb that corporate ladder. The issue with the visual of a ladder is you can either go up or down or get off. There's no space for lateral moves. There's no space for real development. It's also an extremely lonely journey.

These are other common myths we were told our whole lives:

o If you have kids, you can't take risks.

o If you want to get ahead, you need to hustle and grind.

o Once I land my dream job and make $X a year, I'll be happy.

o I must know what I want to do before I consider changing directions.

Trust me, I believed all these myths. I had signs in my office that said, "I'll sleep when I'm dead," and "Everyday I'm hustlin'." I got the job, poured myself into the work, and got the fat check. Guess what, I felt the worst I had felt in my twenty years of working.

———

Why? All the research about burnout points to lack of social support, lack of appreciation and recognition, overwork, and poor self-prioritization. Throwing yourself back onto the hamster wheel will bring you nothing but misery. Ignorance won't be bliss, because this time, you know the difference. But now you have renewed energy and a new perspective on what you want from your work. You have achieved a shift in priorities that allows you longer-term, sustainable progress. As you embark on this next chapter to explore your career steps, let go of the myths and be open.

The remainder of this chapter is filled with tools to help you look forward. Like a spyglass, it is intended to be a resource you can turn to time and time again to identify your goals and explore career or job opportunities.

Define Your Anti-Goals

Revisit your causes of burnout. If you are like me, you burnt out because of the long stressful hours you spent working, you were missing out on relationships, and—let's get real here—you never got clear on your values or your purpose. Keep in mind the environmental conditions that contributed to your burnout.

What are your anti-goals? These are the things you *don't* want to be. Write them down. Here are mine:

I don't want to . . .

- be a reason my family hurts.

- be inauthentic to myself and to others.

- have my physical and mental health suffer.

- neglect spending the time to learn and grow.

- seek external validation as a measure of self-worth.

Define Your Goals

Write a list of goals that are important for you to successfully reenter your work life. These could be very personal based on your past experience. Here are a few common ones:

I would like to have . . .

- greater work/life balance.

- improved personal well-being.

- greater stability and job security.

- mastery—the ability to do what I do best.

- career advancement opportunities, promotion, and project growth.

Now, think about that terrible burned-out feeling you had before your break. Think about that toxic boss or workplace. What were the driving reasons for those feelings? Write them down. Think about the following possibilities to get started:

- You felt micromanaged.

- You felt frustrated by the lack of communication.

- You felt you didn't have control over your job.

- You felt your work wasn't valued or appreciated.

For example, I talked to a C-suite executive who had a negative experience in her last role. She had shifted to a very male-dominated organization that did not align with her values. She was constantly working, she did not feel valued by her peers, and she had little time to spend with her family or children. She made the decision to leave what she felt was a toxic culture. It wasn't because of the hard work or the high-pressure workplace. She had worked in highly demanding roles for three decades. Handling stress wasn't new to her. What finally broke her was that she wanted to feel she was doing her best work, in a collaborative and inclusive team, and that was not happening.

Next, revisit a previous role where you felt excited, where you felt that magical spark. You've probably felt it at some point. What did it look like? What did it feel like? Write it down. Your list might look something like this:

- I felt part of a team achieving a common goal.
- I felt challenged—I was learning something new.
- I felt empowered—I was trusted to make decisions.
- I felt I made an impact—the work I did mattered.

I recently went to coffee with a previous boss, now a mentor and friend, who has opened his own consulting practice. I asked him, "Why the shift to consulting?" He said that for him, he wanted to do work that provided high-impact value to clients that he was uniquely able to deliver. It made me think. We all want to contribute in our own way. We want to feel connected and impactful. I am an optimist who believes that people want to deliver quality work. I think everyone wants work that fills them up. As high-achievers, we want the gold star and kudos.

What are the things you need to go back to work? What does your list of requirements look like? What are your deal-breakers? They could be some of these:

- **Industry**—I want to be in the [fill in the blank] industry.

- **Work/life balance**—I need to be able to work from home and not be required to be accessible on evenings, weekends, and vacations.

- **Mutual impact**—I want to be able to drive impact at the organization.

- **Growth**—I want to be able to learn from my peers, as well as contribute to their learning and expansion.

- **Trust**—I want to be trusted to do my job. I won't be micromanaged.

- **Creativity**—I need a role that will allow me to create something new, not just optimize what's already in place.

- **Diversity and inclusion**—I want to work for a company that values and practices diversity and inclusion.

Choose Your Pace

Keep in mind that where you are in your life now may look very different than it did ten years ago and where you'll be fifteen years from now. You get to choose your pace based your goals and current life situation. This will likely change over time. Remember that when resentment and frustration start to rise within you, something is mismatched. When your professional and personal goals and demands are at odds, you and those around you suffer the most.

To explore where you are, ask yourself a few questions:

- What season of life and career are you in right now? Be sure it creates the right balance for you.

- Are you looking for progression, and if so, what is your ideal timeline for advancement?

- How often do you want to be expected to up-level your skills and expertise during this time in your career?

- What is the level of contribution you are seeking? Do you want to lead from the front or play a supportive role?

Don't Follow Your Passion

Wait. What? People often say to follow your passion. I thought this as well. But I don't think it's passion in the work that really fulfills you. If you think about it, passion can lead to sacrifice, and that sacrifice can lead to burnout. Sure, it could be a sacrifice that sets you up for success later in life. But it can also be the soul-sucking sacrifice that gets you caught in a dead end. Following your passion is terrible career advice. Don't do it.

That's because passion ultimately fades, but your core values and desires will always remain. Growth mindset researcher Carol Dweck and researcher Gregory Walton state this:

> The message to find your passion is generally offered with good intentions, to convey not to worry so much about talent, not to bow to pressure for status or money, and to just find what is meaningful and interesting to you. Unfortunately, the belief system that this message may engender can undermine the very development of people's interests. (Dweck and Walton, 2018)

Professor K. Ann Renninger shared in her research findings that before the age of eight, kids will try anything. Between the ages of eight and twelve, they start to compare themselves with others and become insecure if they're not as good as their peers at something. So around the age of eight, we start to abandon the things that we may be interested in because we aren't good at them. This doesn't mean that we shouldn't pursue career fields in which we won't be successful. But it does mean that in order for us to explore and develop our interests and skills, we need to try new things.

Let Your Regrets Guide You

People regret the things they don't do more than the things they've done. However, I wanted to better understand regret to guide what I would do next. I believe our deepest regret is not reaching our full potential—we regret that we abandoned ourselves, that we are turning into a person we don't recognize anymore. Regret is not just a feeling. It's a reaction to our choices or inaction. And more importantly, regret causes increased stress and negatively impacts our physical health.

A lot of people talk about regret as being "stuck." This regret of inaction cuts deeper. It leads us down the path of anxiety, depression, and a feeling that life could have been different.

A 2008 study shows that Americans' six biggest regrets fall into the following life domains (in descending order of frequency): education, career, romance, parenting, self-improvement, and leisure. The biggest regrets people have are the ones where they see the greatest opportunity. Life regrets are a reflection of where in life people see their most tangible prospects for change, growth, and renewal.

How does regret play into how you want to live your life? Make a list of all the things you regret. Is it a regret of action or inaction? Then, reframe them. What will you do differently to move forward?

- I wish I had gone to law school. → What would it take for me to go to law school?

- I wish I were a better parent. → Make a list of what it means to be a good parent. Then, do the first three things.

- I wish I were a better spouse. → Make a list of what it means to be a better spouse. Then do the first three things.

o I wish I hadn't worked so much. → Then don't. Define what quality work looks like. Focus on impact, not hours. Don't work for yourself? Find a company and boss that values impact over hours.

o I wish I had traveled more. → Plan that trip. Book that flight.

Career Decision-Making

So now you're ready. You're refreshed and you know what your priorities truly are. What the hell do you do now? Throughout the course of your career break, it's likely that ideas have started to float into your mind. What do you want to try? Maybe you want to go back to school. Maybe you start writing that award-winning novel. Whatever those ideas are, conventional or wild, write them down.

For those who are taking a sabbatical and planning to return to their previous companies, this exercise is still relevant. You may be returning to the same workplace, but you are not the same. Maybe you come to the realization that there is a special work project you're interested in, a lateral move opportunity that will help you develop your skills, or a side gig you'd like to explore. You've evolved over the course of your break, and your priorities and needs are different. Honor them, or you risk falling back into burnout.

Steps to Build a Career Matrix

What's a career matrix? It's just a fancy phrase for a chart where you can write down your career ideas, evaluate them based on several factors, and compare them to figure out which ones you want to start on first. The career matrix is intended to help you explore the feasibility of various opportunities. It ensures a close alignment to your core values, while balancing with the logical revenue-generating factors we need to pay the bills.

Follow the steps and fill in the chart (see the Resources section on page 225).

1. Get yourself a notebook and keep it with you wherever you go. Write down all the ideas that come to mind. Remember, there are no bad ideas. It's likely that your off-the-wall ideas could lead to another, more feasible idea. Allow yourself the space to dream.

2. Once you have a good list of ideas, review them. Can you group any of them together? What makes them similar?

3. Pull up your North Star statement from chapter 11.

   ○ Review each idea and rate how much each one aligns with your North Star statement and core values. Use a scale of 1 to 5, with 1 being the lowest and 5 being the highest.

4. In terms of level of difficulty, how would you rate each idea? Would it take an immense amount of effort or would it be relatively simple? Again, rate on the 1-to-5 scale, with 1 being the easiest and 5 being the hardest.

   ○ Review your strengths. Is the idea aligned to your strengths?

   ○ Do you have the skills needed to accomplish this?

5. Would your idea generate revenue?

   ○ Add + for every $50K of estimated revenue.

   ○ Add *ST* for short-term revenue increase, and *LT* for long-term increases.

6. How much would it cost to implement this? Is it an ongoing cost? Or a one-time cost?

○ Add - for every $50K in costs.

○ Add *OT* for one-time costs, *ST* for short-term costs, and *LT* for long-term costs.

7. Score each idea.

○ Each idea is scored across, with core values and level of difficulty serving as the numbers, and the + and – as visual indicators.

○ Note: In the career matrix accessible via the Resources section (page 225), you'll find that it uses weighted scoring. For example, it takes into account that values alignment is more important than level of difficulty. For the purposes of the explanation, I've removed the weighted scoring in the example below.

Career Decision Criteria

Here are a few ideas from my Career Decision Criteria:

	Align with core values (5 highest)	Level of difficulty (5 hardest)	Generate $	Cost $	Total
Apply for corporate marketing leadership roles	3	2	++		5++
Marketing consulting path (independent)	4	3	ST - LT++	-	7++/-
Content creator path and create management content and online community	4	3	ST - LT+	ST - LT ?	7+/--

(continued)

	Align with core values (5 highest)	Level of difficulty (5 hardest)	Generate $	Cost $	Total
Executive and management coach	4	3	ST - LT+	ST -	7+/--
Diversity, equity, and inclusion business coach	4	3	ST - LT+	ST -	7+/--
Give up corporate life and be a meditation instructor	2	4		-	6-
Buy land somewhere and make it a retreat	3	3	?	-	6 -
Live on a cruise ship and work short-term contracts	1	2	-		3 -
Go back to school to be a physician's assistant (bc med school is too long)	2	4	+	-	6+/-
Extend my sabbatical longer, so that I don't have to think about this	2	1	-		3 -

Once you have completed the chart, know that it doesn't have to be perfect. The intention is to use it as a brainstorming exercise to identify what's possible and how and if they align with your North Star statement and core values.

Look at your top three and bottom three. Does anything surprise you? Seeing the numbers line up, is there anything that made you wish the score were higher? What was it? And why do you wish the score were higher?

For some of you, going back to your role at work or finding another corporate role is likely somewhere on the list. Did it score as low or high as you thought it would? Or was it more middle of the road? As I shared in previous chapters, more than 80 percent of people I interviewed and coach will return to their previous companies or find other corporate roles. Not everyone is fleeing the corporate world to switch over to entrepreneurship, and that is perfectly fine. You need to do what is right for you. The difference is that you are intentionally and consciously making decisions that are aligned with your values.

Market Research to Test Your Gut

Once you decide on the one or two paths you are interested in pursuing, test it. As a marketer I am a big fan of market research. Remember that you are exploring these paths, not making a final decision on them. I like to ask myself three questions when considering an opportunity:

1. What do I need to know to decide?

2. Who can I talk to? Who can give me a different perspective?

3. Do I have sufficient information to make a good-enough decision?

Next, check in with how you're feeling. That's right, test how *you* feel. To do this, start taking a little action. Once you identify who to talk to, schedule those lunches or coffees with your network, meet with old colleagues, talk to recruiters. After each encounter, gauge how you're feeling.

Remember the time you spent in the pause phase with its deep focus on listening to your body? When you had to pay attention and notice if you were holding your breath? Use those skills now. When you had lunch with an old colleague and talked about work, did you feel excitement or repulsion? What are your emotions telling you? Use your emotions as a signal to be curious and explore why you are reacting in certain ways.

Yes, sometimes you must do things that you don't want to do. No one really wants to do an interview, but it is a required step to getting a job. There is a difference between damaging self-sacrifice that leads to abandoning yourself and the sacrifice of hard or uncomfortable work required to achieve your dreams and goals. The difference is the end game. Is your hard work or long hours supporting your North Star statement? Test the opportunity by gathering the information needed and ensuring you're listening to your inner voice. Are you pulled toward it or is there a red flag?

Job Seekers: Your Due Diligence

If you've made the decision to leave your workplace and find a new one, it is critical that you thoroughly research and vet the next role, team, and leader you'll work with. The last thing you want is to go into another role and feel burned out within six months. This exercise is about breaking that cycle.

It is common in the interview process to focus on selling yourself. I believe that it must be mutually beneficial. Jobs are not one-sided. So, to ensure that you are the right fit for a new role, you also need to know if the company, the manager, and the position are the right fit for you.

How do you do that? Take your list of potential concerns and non-negotiables for a new role and form questions. Identify who you need to talk to within the organization to get clear and honest answers. Start by finding people you know who work for the company. These are essentially the matchmakers. They know you and they know their company.

- o Want to know if you will be micromanaged? Meet with your peers. If you are very interested in the role, ask the hiring manager if they would be open to you meeting peers. Typically interviews may include a panel, and this will help you assess the culture and management style.

- o Want to know what it's like coming in from a different industry? Ask to meet with someone in the organization who has done the same thing.

- o Want to understand employees' work/life balance? Ask. Don't shy away from the question because you are afraid of how people will react.

- o Want to know about the company's adoption of new ideas? Ask about projects they approved and rejected. Understand the criteria. Understand the decision-makers.

- o When going through your list of questions, be sure to dig in one step deeper with a simple question, "Can you tell me a little more?" The questions you are reviewing are not to check the box but a deep inquiry. For example, the manager may be a good fit for your friend because she is not looking for a coach or mentor. She may prefer a hands-off leader who lets her operate in a silo. That differs from your desire to learn a new role. Be aware of who is giving you feedback and what is important to them.

Stories from Career Breakers

May's Career Exploration

May, the HR leader we shared in the Play chapter, left her role for a six-month career break. During her six months, she focused on the play, pause, and plan phases. She rested, she spent time with her family and animals, and she was intentional about how she would return to work. After her break, May found a company that balanced her professional aspirations and her personal fulfillment. She re-entered the workforce, taking a director-level role that allowed for more flexible time. Her re-entry was intentional and aligned to what was important to her.

She said, "While not all of us have the luxury of taking the time off, I do hope people are taking measures for more balance by being strict about their time, disengaging from work to be fully present for the good stuff, and even changing jobs for a clean new start."

Taylor's Time Off

I met Taylor on LinkedIn. His story is similar to most of ours. As a senior-level leader, he often found himself working twelve- to fourteen-hour days. He deprioritized his time with his kids, and the stress continued to compound daily. He was so distracted that his kids felt as if they were a burden to him. When he made the decision to take a four-month career break, he shifted his outlook. He said, "This break taught me my worth and the value of my time. Work cannot come before mental health and family." For Taylor, he is in a season of ensuring that he is focused on his family and kids. Today, he's found a role where he can find balance, be there for his kids' activities, and be more present.

Emilia's Journey

Emilia was a VP at a top national brand when she decided to leave with nothing lined up. She was burned out, exhausted, and unfulfilled. She took two months off and prioritized taking care of herself. When she was ready, Emilia accepted an SVP role at a company that prioritized well-being. She said to me, "I can tell you, beyond a shadow of a doubt, I made the right decision." Today, she is operating with her mojo back and she's found the balance of doing great work while living a great life. She said to me, "These companies do exist! There are workplaces with the work culture that cares about its employees—where meaningful work and work/life balance are attainable."

My Story: How I Figured Out My Next Move

I took my break, and now I was ready for hard work. My mom is a highly determined woman who has been the top salesperson for a cosmetics line at Macy's for the past thirty-plus years. Growing up, I remember sitting behind the cosmetics counter coloring or doing extra math homework while she worked. I'd go to work with her and do my own eight-hour shift, doing worksheets, wandering the mall, and getting Auntie Annie's Pretzels with my mom. She taught me the value of hard work and achievement. Deep down, she was competitive with herself, increasing her own sales targets day after day, month after month. All this was passed down to me. I was in the game to beat myself. My next step was no different. I needed to believe that I could make any of my career paths happen.

It will probably come as a surprise to you that I left my well-paying, nice-title job with nothing lined up. Especially because though I am completely comfortable taking risks that I feel are achievable, I am averse to *big* risks. That comes from my immigrant parents who told me to always have a plan. But in this case, I felt as if I could go down several paths. Some would be more financially comfortable than others, and all would require some hard work.

Putting the Career Matrix into Action

On page 185, I shared an example of my career break matrix. In order to complete that matrix, I started by writing down my ideas. I had a few tracks that I could explore based on my background and expertise that seemed reasonable:

1. Professor

2. Executive and management coach

3. Host a podcast and be a content creator

4. Open my own marketing consulting practice

5. Diversity, equity, and inclusion business coach

6. Find a corporate executive role and lead marketing functions

But I also included my totally off-the-wall ideas:

7. Write a book

8. Move to Hawaii

9. Buy a farm or a ranch

10. Go work at a nonprofit

11. Take the LSATs and go to law school

12. Open a coffee shop/coworking space

13. Be a physician's assistant (even off-the-wall me knew med school was too long)

14. Live on a cruise ship and work short-term contracts

15. Give up corporate life and be a meditation instructor

16. Extend my sabbatical longer, so I didn't have to think about it

I'm not going to lie to you, even my off-the-wall ideas looked appealing and doable. Some were way bigger financial risks than others, and some seemed more difficult. How would I live on a cruise ship with a toddler? To be fair, people do it. What was critical was how did these career opportunities align with my personal values and the life I was designing and creating?

I filled in the Career Decision Criteria with these sixteen ideas and scored them. When it came to deciding what I was going to do next, I knew I had four primary interests that would align with my core values and my desires. I gave myself the freedom to change my mind, but these were the areas I gravitated to:

Marketing Consulting—Score: 7++/-

Consulting could give me the freedom to expand by building something new and help fuel that curious problem-solver/scientist within me. Because it was mine, it would be an authentic representation of who I am and how I want to contribute to the world. The start-up cost financially would be relatively low. I'd start with networking and identifying past colleagues or organizations who would need my services.

Coaching—Score: 7+/- -

Executive/leadership coaching and diversity, equity, and inclusion coaching were tied for me, so I combined them into one. I want to help organizations operate effectively and efficiently but also deliver value to their employees, not just shareholders. I could blend coaching with my consulting business. At the time of creating my criteria chart, I felt that the revenue generation would not be strong. So because of that reason, I deprioritized this one.

In my career decision criteria, finding another corporate role was the safe path at that stage in my life. It scored 5 points. But I felt drawn to trying something different. I needed to bet on myself. Based on my career decision matrix, I decided to pursue the two that sounded most appealing— opening my own marketing consulting practice and engaging in coaching on the side. This would help fulfill both of my desires.

There is no right or wrong way to do this. Your path is *your path*. The key is to use the criteria map to help you identify objectively what *you* want to do. It outlines all the options and helps you realize that even though something may be "off the wall," it doesn't mean that it is unachievable. So if you have a passion project you have wanted to work on, add it to the list and see where it stacks up.

Free Diving

- Complete the career matrix exercise to start mapping out your next career paths.

- Write down your list of requirements for your next role. What are your deal-breakers?

- If you are interviewing for another role, identify what questions you would ask to evaluate if the organization, manager, and culture would support your North Star statement and core values.

Part 3

Disembarkment: Life on Land

CHAPTER 13

Pursue: Moving Forward

*"No man ever steps in the same river twice, for it's not
the same river and he's not the same man."*

—*Heraclitus*

I imagine that when my parents were drifting in the middle of the ocean, the sea pitch black, they were filled with hope and fear simultaneously. They would tell me the fear of that night, the fear of the unknown. They'd follow the stars until they saw land. There, the time moved slow. Minutes felt like hours. Days felt like weeks. Weeks felt like years. However, the hope for a better life pushed them forward.

My journey is not the same voyage my parents made. Theirs was one of survival and hope for a better future. That hope burned a fire bright and deep within me. What we share is that I also want to create a better world for my daughter. For me, the changes were inside out.

Change often happens one small degree at a time. This sabbatical or career break is a commitment to transformation. As the Heraclites quote at the beginning of this chapter shows, we are constantly evolving and changing. And that is the beauty of life.

When I think about transformation, I often find myself pulled to the Ship of Theseus. According to the legend, Theseus defeats King Minos and rescues the children of Athens, escaping onto a ship toward Delos. Each year, Athenians commemorate this by taking the ship on a pilgrimage to Delos. Over centuries of maintenance, each individual part of the ship is replaced—plank by plank. This leads us to the paradox: Is it the same ship?

As we think about ourselves over time, we are constantly evolving. We're gaining new skills and learning from each of our experiences. Use the skills you've learned in the play, pause, and plan phases as some of your tools moving forward. It is important to periodically re-evaluate the path you are on and adjust your plan and goals when needed.

We've spent the majority of this book resetting, recharging, and redefining what we want in life. In this section we focus on life after your break—the step where you go out there and pursue it!

In part 3, we'll review three important areas:

1. How to deal with your sea legs—transitioning back into the world of work

2. Handling headwinds—dealing with setbacks

3. Navigating life on land—creating systems to help you avoid new burnout

Your Sea Legs

When I was in grade school, my family had a boat that we would take out on Table Rock Lake in Missouri. I recall a time we were out on the lake over the July Fourth weekend and it was packed. As we rode out trying to find a nice cove to hang out in, the bow of the boat kept bobbing up and down from the waves of all the other boats. Sitting at the front, I was gripping the railings as we slammed into each wave. Later that night, I could still feel the waves in my chest and gut, swaying inside as I lay in my bed.

That is how you'll feel upon re-entry. Things look and feel different, and you're trying to get your bearings. It's perfectly normal. You've spent time over the last few weeks refocusing your priorities. You have a different perspective and a new sense of clarity.

There are a few ways to help manage your sea legs.

1. **Gentle movements:** Take your time. It is tempting to start sprinting after you've had this time off. You'll feel the pressure to go do something urgently. Resist that urge. Slow things down to be sure that you are acting from a place of clarity, not panic.

2. **Stay calm:** The anxiety can make it worse. In the pause phase, you learned techniques to help you manage your anxiety and identify ways to settle back into yourself.

3. **Focus on a fixed point:** In order to reorient your inner sense of balance and bring you back to stability, you need to refocus on what you have gained during this break. Staying true to yourself, your values, and your vision for life are critical. Focus on your North Star statement to keep you grounded.

Life happens. Whether it's during your break, immediately after your break, or even years later, we need to find ways to be resilient to what storms life may bring. I struggled with this deeply. It was easy to try to sprint again. I had a ton of energy stored from my months of rest. I was ready to go! The issue was that my desire to sprint ahead came rooted in my desire to somehow make up for the time I felt I had lost in this break. I was so wrong.

Your career break is the deepest gift you gave to yourself. Embrace it and give yourself the grace to emerge from the time off with the same intention you went into it.

Headwinds

We live in a world where productivity is valued over rest. Our industrial society prioritizes production and transaction over humanity. Workplaces and thus our networks reward achievement and status. I am no stranger to the desire to win that trophy or earn that gold star. It's easy to slip into old habits.

I met with a friend during the plan phase of my career break. She talked about her company's new investors and the strong need for her, her boss, and all her colleagues to prove themselves. They wanted to show two things: "I am good enough to be here" and "We'll exceed performance results, whatever it takes." I felt my head nod, the typical response I would have given just twelve weeks before. I knew exactly what she was talking about because I had spent every day of the past twenty years doing that—doing whatever it took to perform at the highest levels. After our coffee chat, I sat back and reflected. I felt uneasy, almost angry. Here was this incredibly brilliant and high-achieving woman feeling like she needed to prove her worth, her intellect, and her capabilities. The New Me knew there was more, and I needed more from my work.

Business leaders are not immune. My friend Sean and I worked together at a marketing agency in Kansas City. He was an SVP of marketing before he founded his own marketing agency. For ten years, Sean and I joked that we have the "work disease," the desire to put in incessant hours. When I was exploring my own marketing consulting practice, I went to Sean. One Friday afternoon, we sat in his office with eyes wide open. Life changed our perspective. This disease was nothing to be proud of. We said to ourselves, "We're smart people. How did others figure it out so much earlier than we did?" How did they figure out that life, love, and family were the most important?

Your desire to put in the hours, to react to the emails and text messages on weekends, the rush of a fire to put out— that temptation will be there. You must decide how you want to react to it. When you pride yourself on being a workaholic, what happens when you remove the badge?

I was talking to a friend who was preparing to return to her work after a three-month break. She joked that she wished she had followed my four *P*'s path. She wasn't ready to come back. She had enjoyed the time to rest and rejuvenate. She had spent the past three months prioritizing her health and her family. And now, as she was describing her return, she was nervous what it would do to her well-being. She juggled between being that high-achieving, get-it-done person, who was also advocating for her team and her peers. As she shared what she wanted to achieve upon her return, she was battling herself—how do I take care of my health while throwing myself into another fire again? You get clear on your values, you prioritize what's important, and set your expectations and your boundaries accordingly.

––––––––––

The world is full of triggers and messages that may not align with your goals. You may find yourself back on the road to burnout. So, what do you do about it? You recognize it. You learn from it. And you intentionally do something different.

We have a lot of unlearning to do during our career break, and it will take time and a few missteps to get there. In your journey, it is inevitable that you will face some headwinds and find yourself drifting back to old habits.

So what do you do when you relapse? For me, it was about a R-E-S-E-T.

R: Recognition. Recognize the behavior. I didn't see my relapses until I was deep in them. The key is to monitor your mind and your body. Did you just default back to the "old you"?

E: Environment. Find an environment where you feel safe to explore your emotions and recenter yourself again. For me there are a few places I feel safe: home, my car, and the library. You may have your own preferred spaces.

S: Set boundaries. Know what your triggers are and set healthy boundaries to protect yourself. You have 100 percent permission to do whatever you need. The word *no* was the greatest gift I gave myself. Setting boundaries and saying no meant putting away the phone and not responding to texts or emails until certain days or a certain time. This may sound crazy, but I said to myself, "I'm not going to check my email until Tuesday." And I needed to be good with that.

E: Empathy. Show yourself empathy and self-compassion. It's not too late; you can just start over again, whether it's the next moment, next hour, or the next day.

T: Take a time-out. I needed to take a time-out to reflect and meditate. It was important to recenter myself. I went to a work-related meeting that I just wasn't emotionally ready for. I thought, "Surely, enough time has passed, I'm good." I'll tell you that the rush of anxiety didn't come until several hours after. And then, I found myself on the treadmill, heart racing faster than it should for a walk. I got off the treadmill, found a hiding spot in the vacant yoga studio, and meditated for ten minutes. I needed to put myself in time-out and take what I needed.

There is no such thing as perfection in this life or in this journey that we are on. Don't beat yourself up. It is just part of the process.

I'm not really an athlete, and I don't sport. But let's just go with this analogy for a minute. When you're playing tennis, it's you and the other player. You're volleying the ball back and forth, back and forth. You're present and aware. You miss the ball you should have easily been able to hit. You get frustrated. "I can't believe I let that happen. One more miss and I'll lose this set," you say to yourself. You serve the ball. "Okay, not bad, but could have been better," the voice in your head says. It bounces back to you. "Don't miss it this time," the voice says. And guess what, you do.

You are not your thoughts. And that inner critic in your head is not you. Meditation has taught me the most important lesson—to sit with that voice, but not react to it, and not let it impact me. I acknowledge it and move on.

So let's imagine if we were playing the game a little differently. When you miss the ball again, your voice comes in, "I can't believe I let that happen. One more miss and I'll lose this set," it says. This time, acknowledge that voice. Then, take three seconds. Breathe in. Fill those lungs, and feel your chest inflate. Then push that air out with a sigh. You can feel your chest deflate, and your ribs sink in. Allow yourself that space to sink into your body. Just drop into it. Serve that ball. Then breathe in, then out. Just stay in your body. Return the ball. Watch it be returned. Volley it back. This time, your opponent misses your return.

That's all it takes. We are imperfect, but we can reframe and change. We don't have to let the voice inside us dictate who we are or how we live. I have spent thirty-nine years stuck in my head. I prided myself for always thinking with my head and not my heart. "I am not an emotional person," I would say, "I am logical." To be the most authentic person, it is often illogical. The place where authenticity resides is in our heart.

Systems for Success

*"Wisdom is knowing when to have rest, when to have
activity, and how much of each to have."*
—Sri Sri Ravi Shankar

During your career break, you had the benefit of being a little more insulated and isolated than you would if you were working. You didn't have daily "work" adding to your list of competing interests. Those tiny stresses that would build up have been diminished. No Slack alerts. No late night emails from clients, your teammates, or your boss. No juggling a hundred balls in the air. As you disembark from the career break, you'll be faced with many competing interests. Systems and frameworks are how you survive and make continued progress on your well-being.

In this chapter, I share a variety of tools that you can use when needed. Go to the Resources on page 225 to access the link to download all the Systems for Success templates.

Time Management

In moments of overwhelm and constant juggling, it is easy to focus on ensuring nothing falls.

- o **Time audits** is the exercise of reviewing how you are spending your time in fifteen-minute increments for a week. Don't use your calendar of what meetings you have, mark down the actual activities. You'll find a spreadsheet in the Resources section on page 225.

- o **Ideal weeks** involves taking the same spreadsheet for your time audit and creating the schedule you desire. This could entail working on certain projects on certain days, or breaking your days into blocks. As you will recall, this is how we planned our career break.

- o **Time blocking** involves scheduling specific blocks of time for different tasks or activities throughout the day. I borrowed the concept of block scheduling from Charlie Gilkey. He breaks down four different types of blocks.

  - Focus (90–120 minutes): Time where you're especially creative, inspired, and able to do high-level work that requires focus.

  - Admin (30–60 minutes): Lower-energy blocks of time where you're not in the zone to do the work that requires heavy lifting, but there are still other types of work you can do effectively. I think of this as email or return phone call time.

  - Social (90–120 minutes): Time where you're primed and energetically in the right space to meet with people.

- Recovery (variable): Time that you use for exercise, meditation, and self-care.

o The **Pomodoro Technique** involves breaking work into twenty-five-minute focused intervals (called Pomodoros) followed by a short break.

o **Sprint planning** involves reviewing what can be completed in two weeks based on the number of hours in those two weeks. It takes your ideal work week and timeboxing exercise and makes it a habit. Being a digital marketer who has worked with developers for most my career, sprint planning on work projects and life projects has been critical.

Decision Fatigue

We make thirty-five thousand decisions a day. That's right: from the moment you wake up until you fall asleep, your brain is constantly making decisions. No wonder you are exhausted. And when you are drained, you make poor decisions.

A 2011 Columbia Business School research study of criminal parole approvals found that the time of day had a significant impact on judges' decisions. The research shows that judges would give a favorable ruling in the morning 65 percent of the time. However, as the day proceeded, the likelihood of a criminal getting a favorable ruling dropped to zero. Based on the 1,100 cases, it did not matter the crime—murder, rape, theft, embezzlement—a criminal was more likely to get a positive parole hearing response if it was scheduled in the morning and after food breaks than at the end of a long day.

To help combat decision fatigue, focus on three areas: automate, eliminate, and prioritize.

Automate

- o **Morning routine:** First simplify your morning routing by getting up at the same time and having the same breakfast.

- o **Set up recurring grocery delivery:** Once you've standardized your meals, scheduling (a.k.a. delegating) grocery orders becomes super easy. Same cart, every week.

- o **Simplify your wardrobe:** No one likes standing in front of a closet saying, "I have nothing to wear." Standardize your wardrobe with your basics, and then zhuzh it up if desired. Same goes for your kids too! My daughter has a uniform, also known as Spider-Man clothes. Pick a shirt, pick pants, let's go.

Eliminate

- o **Get rid of the clutter:** If you're like me, I have way too much crap—clothes I haven't worn in years, kid clothes that don't fit anymore, toys that need to be purged.

- o **Get rid of activities/tasks:** We live in a society that believes more is better. However, the more you add to your life, the more decisions you make, and the more draining on your energy and time it is. Hobbies, activities, and volunteering are all wonderful, but if you need to take a break from them, do it. If your kid signed up for five activities after school, eliminate three or more.

Prioritize

- o **Eisenhower Matrix:** One system that I find myself using is the Eisenhower Matrix. President Dwight

Eisenhower developed the concept to help him prioritize high-stakes issues throughout his career from US Army general to the president of the United States. Create a four-quadrant table. Label the columns Urgent and Not Urgent and the rows Important and Not Important. The quadrant where Urgent and Important intersect = do now; Important/Not Urgent = defer; Urgent/Not Important = Delegate; Not Important/Not Urgent = delete.

o **Value vs. Effort** allows you to plot tasks based on the effort required and the benefit generated. A visual plot aids you in prioritizing high-value, low-effort tasks and removing low-value tasks.

o **10/10/10 Rule** has you reflect on how a decision will make you feel in ten minutes, ten months, and ten years from now. This promotes long-term thinking in decision-making.

Regular Alignment Check-Ins

When was the last time you re-created a strategic plan for your life? Do you schedule weekly one-on-ones with yourself, your spouse, or your family? What's interesting to me is that we spend a lot of time in the corporate world creating strategies, initiatives, and check-ins, but we rarely do it in our own lives. Don't deprioritize yourself and your life any longer.

Daily

o Schedule thirty minutes throughout the day for meditation to pause.

o Move for thirty to forty-five minutes daily.

Weekly

- Schedule a weekly play date. Treat your weekends like short vacations.

- Schedule time to do nothing. If you want to enjoy life, you need to not be in constant motion.

Monthly

- Look back. Reflect on the past month of what went well and what didn't.

- Look forward. How would you build your ideal month looking ahead? Ensure this aligns with your core values.

Quarterly

- Schedule check-ins with yourself on a quarterly basis. Review your core values, your goals, your well-being. Then identify what you want to start, stop, or continue doing.

- Explore a life audit to evaluate whether your career, relationships, or lifestyle are aligned with your core values (see more in the Resource section, page 225).

Annually

- Annually create core values and goals, similar to your work-performance goals. Review and reflect on how you are prioritizing what is important for a fulfilling life. Living your life on purpose means being intentional with how you spend your time.

Stories from Career Breakers

Riley: The Juggler

My client Riley is a VP with two kids who are in grade school. When we first met, I asked her the question I always start coaching calls with: "How are you doing?" "Struggling," was her response. Riley had been at her company for eight years. She was known as the "fixer" at work. If a project was delayed, if something was broken, if something was critical, it went to Riley. Over time, it sucked everything out of her. In the past year, she had noticed that things at home were starting to show signs of cracks. Her kids were struggling in school and with friends. After a family vacation, she noticed just how tough things were for her kids. They were disconnected. Something had to change. That was the catalyst for her career break.

Riley's career break was focused on three priorities: (1) Ensuring time for her rest, (2) being present for her kids, and (3) identifying systems to help support her. What I love about Riley's story is that she was not scared to ask for help. She is a solver. She could clearly identify the chaos in her schedule, in her environment, and internally. She also could prioritize what she needed to work on, to allow herself space to focus on others. She had the Eisenhower Matrix in her brain. She delegated and outsourced groceries, cleaning, and tutoring support. This allowed her to focus on her key strengths—bringing her presence and focus to situations where it was needed.

Elle's Story

Elle has worked in marketing for more than twenty years in large-scale organizations. When she decided to take a career break, she knew that she needed to prioritize work and life differently at this stage in her life. She needed to set boundaries to refocus her energy for her family and herself. Elle clearly communicated what she could bring to her new role, as well as what she needed—work/life balance with maximum weekly hours. After her break, she found a company that valued her contributions and her boundaries. In our conversations, her approach to boundary setting was smooth and without guilt. It was refreshing to hear her approach.

The fastest form of erosion is that of moving water. Don't believe me? Look at the Grand Canyon. Physical erosion occurs fastest on steep surfaces. But emotional erosion is dramatically impacted by soil type (your foundation) and heavy storms (life events). This is the compounded impact of burnout. You feel as if everything falls apart all at once. If you are like Riley and Elle, you are juggling a million things simultaneously and your to-do list is endless.

Author Nora Roberts once said, "The key to juggling is to know that some of the balls you have in the air are made of plastic and some are made of glass. And if you drop a plastic ball, it bounces, no harm done. If you drop a glass ball, it shatters, so you have to know which balls are glass and which are plastic and prioritize catching the glass ones."

It will feel impossible to juggle everything. Follow Nora Roberts's advice and identify which balls are plastic and which are glass. I'll give you a hint: your family, your relationships, your health, those are the glass balls. The next step is to clearly communicate what your boundaries are. Elle is a prime example of this.

Free Diving

- Review the play, pause, and plan chapters again. Similar to your break, schedule when you will have a play date, a pause date, and a planning session. I like to ensure I have play on the calendar weekly, pause daily, and plan quarterly.

- List all the balls you are juggling. Then categorize them into glass balls versus plastic balls.

- Write down how you will build resilience. What are one or two ways to help you?

- Review the list of Systems and Frameworks, and identify one or two that you would like to try.

CHAPTER 14

Take the Leap

"A ship is always safe at shore.
But that is not what it is built for."

—*Albert Einstein*

I Am Your Personal Hype Woman, Cheerleader, and Coach

As you've probably figured out by now, I have never been a great hype woman for myself, but I'm pretty good at taking on that role to help others. So my hype to you is this:

Seize this time and opportunity!

What's been holding you back? Before I started down this path, I kept making excuses. "I'll do _____ when I have time, when I have more money, when my kids are older, when I get there . . ." That, of course, got me nowhere.

If you have the same narrative floating around in your brain, keep this in mind: we get only this one life. So, stop wasting time and make a collective commitment to create your best life right now. Create your when today and every day.

Walt Disney said, "The way to get started is to quit talking and begin doing."

So get out there. Take the leap.

I will leave you with these final takeaways:

Plan for your career break to start within twelve months. When I first started thinking about it, my exit plan started in five years, which was a mistake. It was too far away and I felt the effects of it every day that passed. Make it sooner. Whether it's a sabbatical or a transition from your role, or a clean break, find a way to make it happen within one year. We humans love short-term gratification, so give yourself that gift. Besides, if you picked up this book, you've already been thinking about it. Make your plan today. Go to Resources (page 225) to access my Career Break Checklist to help you prepare.

Let go of what others think. This is really hard. For many people, taking a career break is at odds with what society tells us defines success. You can be intentional and prepared when taking time off. You've financially, mentally, emotionally, and physically prepared for a career break. Let go of other's misconceptions. It's normal to feel that anxiety in your gut, acknowledge it, and name it. But then hop in your boat and sail away—play is just over the horizon.

Keep your eyes forward. When you head off on this adventure of self-exploration or soul deepening, you may feel tempted in the beginning to just turn around. It's a little dark, a little scary, and there's a whole ocean out there. The fear might start to set in. Good. What's on the other side of that fear is you. Keep sailing!

Stay curious. A guiding quote in my life has been Albert Einstein's "I have no special talents. I am only passionately curious." As you explore your life ahead, stay curious. Pay attention to what your mind and body are telling you. Feel the pull of that interesting conversation that may lead to something bigger and better. Pay attention and ask yourself, "What should I learn here?"

You are never truly lost. At some point as you are floating around the in-between of your break, you'll feel anxious, lost, and overwhelmed. There may be days that are idle, and you won't know how to fill them. Your Outlook or Google calendar will feel empty, and you might feel as if you've lost your identity. It's going to be fine. I felt that too. Take a moment to pause. Breathe. Meditate. You have permission to be here. You did the work; you made a plan; now go out there and live it!

I'll be here cheering you on!

CHAPTER 15

Be a New Kind of Leader

*"We are like islands in the sea, separate on
the surface but connected on the deep."*

—*William James*

I've spent the bulk of this book talking about what individuals can do to help recover from burnout; however, it would be remiss if I didn't share the other accountable party to burnout: the organizations and companies we work for. You alone are not responsible for your burnout. And as you re-enter the workplace, it is critical that you first understand this, and second, that you play a role in minimizing future burnout for yourself and others.

Imagine a canary in a coal mine. It comes out sick and covered in soot. We don't look at the canary and say, "What's wrong with the canary?" We blame the environment, not the individual. What are the conditions at work that are causing us to be sick?

Burnout is systemic. The leading causes of burnout within organizations are poor management, employees not connecting to the corporate strategy, and a negative workplace culture. And management is the driving challenge.

In a 2023 poll by *Fortune*, 64 percent of people said they have experienced a toxic workplace, and 44 percent of them blamed leadership. Toxic workplaces impact your well-being. In fact, people who work in toxic workplaces are three times more likely to say they experience harm to their mental health at work. This is not the way that we should be working.

Of the people that I have worked with in coaching and interviewed as part of this book, there are common trends in the contributions to their burnout. Burnout is both the responsibility of the person and the organization. Burnout expert and psychology professor emerita Christina Maslach says there are six mismatches between workers and their jobs that predict burnout:

- Work overload

- Lack of control

- Insufficient rewards

- Socially toxic workplace community

o Absence of fairness

o Values conflict

You know these mismatches all too well. You've likely experienced them firsthand and felt powerless in shielding your teams from these. We've been part of organizations that embody the characteristics we desire—high impact, alignment with our values, collaborative community, and fairness in pay, workload, and rewards. Through your play, pause, and plan sessions, you are now able to see a little more clearly. We know what we don't want, what leader we don't want to be, and what organization we won't be part of.

We are in a time of opportunity, and you are uniquely positioned to be able to change how we work and live. It is a different vision for a different type of work culture, one that people are desperately seeking.

You have the power to make an impact in your organizations and communities. More than 80 percent of the people I coach re-enter the workforce. The difference is that when they return, they are now leading organizations as people who have a clearer vision of what they want from life and from work. They know the impact and costs of burnout. They know what it feels like to be unappreciated by their boss. They know what it feels like to not be valued.

If you are in a leadership role in your company, you can make meaningful changes that will help your colleagues and anyone you manage avoid the burnout that drove you out of the office in the first place. If you aren't in a formal leadership role, you are equipped with knowing how to prevent burnout for others.

You can create impactful change.

What Is the Kind of Work Culture You Want to Create?

I believe that being a leader and specifically someone's manager is the most meaningful work you can do. You have the ability to impact people's lives on a daily basis. You can be the best boss or coach they ever had. Or you could be the nightmare they cannot wait to leave.

Take a lesson in leadership from orcas. That's right, these whales can teach us a lot about leadership. Like humans, orcas are social and problem-solving beings. They live and travel in pods and have created a culture that focuses on growth. They hunt in groups where every member plays a role. They communicate. And they encourage learning. Scientists have documented orcas training their younger whales to try new things. Be an orca.

To start you on the road to positive and lasting change in the workplace, here are some commitments I would ask you to make:

1. **Be intentional.** You get to define how you want to live and work. As you lead your teams, be sure that you customize solutions that are rooted in their feedback. There is no one-size-fits-all solution, so get intentional about the problem you are solving and the solution you propose. Remember, your actions will serve as models for your team and others.

2. **Embrace mistakes.** We will make mistakes if we try new things. Low-trust, toxic cultures are created when organizations point fingers and don't embrace learning. Embracing mistakes also means removing the stigma that failure is a sign of weakness. Create an environment that removes the fear of being negatively viewed for speaking up or asking for help.

3. **Offer control.** I believe that leaders and managers have the ability to make or break their team. An empathetic and compassionate leader is invested in the person, not just productivity. Empathy is not simply listening, but also action. Control and autonomy are critical for people's work life. Allowing people to manage their work—where, when, how, and with whom—can help effectively empower employees.

4. **Give credit and appreciation.** One of the top drivers of burnout is a lack of appreciation and credit. Celebrate your team's efforts and successes. Spend the time to appreciate your team and personalize your appreciation.

5. **Show up as your authentic values-driven self.** The greatest gift you can bring into this world is your authentic self. It gives everyone else permission to do the same. And imagine, if we all were coming from a place of authenticity, what kind of work and life we could create.

In my world of work, we wouldn't experience burnout because of the weight of the work. Instead, we'd create organizations that positively contribute to people's lives outside of just a paycheck. Where people could come together, solve problems, learn, and accomplish together. People want to feel valued, that their work matters. That they matter. Imagine a world where we could communicate what we needed at work and in our lives.

You have the power to re-enter the workplace clearer, more intentional, and with dignity. You are rested, recovered, and ready to go! I have no doubt that as a high achiever, you will continue to find roles that offer you leadership opportunities. Use your newfound perspective to create more balanced and well-being-focused organizations and teams. Consider how you will model work/life balance in your organization. How will you demonstrate appreciation and gratitude to your team? How will you foster growth? How will you lead with authenticity and empathy?

Designing an organization that focuses both on profitability and personal well-being is the new normal. That is the corporate work culture I am working to change and create. I hope you'll be part of that change too.

May you have fair winds and following seas.

Resources

In this book, I've shared numerous models and resources to help you prepare for a career break. Access the Career Break Checklist, workbooks for your planning process, schedules during your break, and more!

Use the QR code or visit careerbreakcompass.com to access all the recommended resources and templates for your career break plan.

Looking for a Community?

So am I. Let's create it together.

_____

Visit careerbreakcompass.com to access a community for those on a career break. It is intended to help create a community of life creators—all of you who are defining your purpose and making your communities, workplaces, and selves better.

References

Achor, S., Gielan, M., Kopans, D., & Molinsky, A. (2017, June 29). *Burnout at Work Isn't Just About Exhaustion. It's Also About Loneliness.* Harvard Business Review. Retrieved April 14, 2023, from https://hbr.org/2017/06/burnout-at-work-isnt-just-about-exhaustion-its-also-about-loneliness.

American Psychological Association. (n.d.). *Psychology.* APA Dictionary of Psychology. Retrieved April 13, 2023, from https://dictionary.apa.org/burnout.

Baranik, L., Wang, M., Gong, Y., & Shi, J. (2014, September). Customer Mistreatment, Employee Health and Job Performance: Cognitive Rumination and Social Sharing as Mediating Mechanisms. *Journal of Management.* SSRN. 10.1177/0149206 314550995.

Begley, S. (2007). *Train Your Mind, Change Your Brain: How a New Science Reveals Our Extraordinary Potential to Transform Ourselves.* Random House Publishing Group.

Brown, S. L., & Vaughan, C. (2010). *Play: How It Shapes the Brain, Opens the Imagination, and Invigorates the Soul.* Penguin Publishing Group.

Bureau of Labor Statistics, U.S. Department of Labor, The Economics Daily, Men spent 5.6 hours per day in leisure and sports activities, women 4.9 hours, in 2021 at https://www.bls .gov/opub/ted/2022/men-spent-5-6-hours-per-day-in -leisure-and-sports-activities-women-4-9-hours-in-2021.htm (visited September 9, 2023).

Byrd-Craven, J., Geary, D. C., Rose, A. J., & Ponzi, D. (2008, March). Co-ruminating increases stress hormone levels in women. *Hormones and Behavior, 53*(3), 489–492. ScienceDirect. https://doi.org/10.1016/j.yhbeh.2007.12.002.

Cameron, J. (2016). *The Artist's Way: 30th Anniversary Edition.* Penguin Publishing Group.

Centers for Disease Control and Prevention. (2018, February 13). *Products - Data Briefs - Number 303 - February 2018*. Centers for Disease Control and Prevention. Retrieved April 13, 2023, from https://www.cdc.gov/nchs/products/databriefs/db303.htm.

Covey, S. R. (1989). *The Seven Habits of Highly Effective People*. Simon and Schuster.

Dalton-Smith, S. (2017). *Sacred Rest: Recover Your Life, Renew Your Energy, Restore Your Sanity*. FaithWords.

Dare to Lead | List of Values - Brené Brown. (n.d.). Brene Brown. Retrieved April 13, 2023, from https://brenebrown.com/resources/dare-to-lead-list-of-values/.

Delroisse, S., Rime, B., & Stinglhamber, F. (2022, May 5). Quality of social sharing of emotions alleviates job burnout: The role of meaning of work. *Journal of Health Psychology*, *28*(1), 61–76. Sage Journals. https://doi.org/10.1177/135910532 21091039.

Dunatchik, A., Gerson, K., Glass, J., Jacobs, J. A., & Stritzel, H. (2021). Gender, Parenting, and the Rise of Remote Work During the Pandemic: Implications for Domestic Inequality in the United States. *Gender & Society*, *35*(2), 194–205. Retrieved April 4, 2023, from https://journals.sagepub.com/doi/10.1177/0891243221001301.

Dweck, C., & Walton, G.M. (2018). Implicit Theories of Interest: Finding Your Passion or Developing It? *Psychological Science*, *29*(10), 1653–1664. Sage Journals. https://doi.org/10.1177/0956 797618780643.

The Employee Burnout Crisis: Study Reveals Big Workplace Challenge in 2017. (2017, January 9). Business Wire. Retrieved April 14, 2023, from https://www.businesswire.com/news/home/20170109005377/en/The-Employee-Burnout-Crisis-Study-Reveals-Big-Workplace-Challenge-in-2017.

Exercise can boost your memory and thinking skills. (2021, February 15). Harvard Health. Retrieved April 13, 2023, from https://www.health.harvard.edu/mind-and-mood/exercise-can-boost-your-memory-and-thinking-skills

Eyerman, J. (2013). A Clinical Report of Holotropic Breathwork in 11,000 Psychiatric Inpatients in a Community Hospital Setting. *MAPS Bulletin Special Edition*, *23*(1), 24–27.

Farber, B. (1990). Burnout in Psychotherapists: Incidence, Types, and Trends. *Psychotherapy in Private Practice, 8*(1), 35–44. https://www.researchgate.net/publication/232566633_Burnout_in _Psychotherapists_Incidence_Types_and_Trends.

Fields, J. (2021). *Sparked: Discover Your Unique Imprint for Work That Makes You Come Alive.* HarperCollins Publishers.

Gilkey, C. (2019). *Start Finishing: How to Go from Idea to Done.* Sounds True.

Harter, J. (2021, November 15). *The Loneliest Employees.* Gallup. Retrieved April 14, 2023, from https://www.gallup.com/work place/357386/loneliest-employees.aspx.

Hersey, T. (2022). *Rest Is Resistance: A Manifesto.* Little, Brown Spark.

Holmes, S. W., Morris, R., Clance, P. R., & Putney, R. T. (1996). Holotropic Breathwork: An experiential approach to psychotherapy. *Psychotherapy Theory Research Practice Training, 33*(1), 114–120. ResearchGate. https://www.researchgate.net /publication/232555956_Holotropic_breathwork_An _experiential_approach_to_psychotherapy.

Houillon, A., Lorenz, R. C., Boehmer, W., & Rapp, M.A. (2013). Chapter 21 - The effect of novelty on reinforcement learning. *Progress in the Brain, 202,* 415–439. Science Direct. https://www .sciencedirect.com/science/article/abs/pii/B9780444626042 000216?via%3Dihub.

Huang, J., Krivkovich, A., Starikova, I., & Yee, L. (2022, October 18). *Women in the Workplace.* McKinsey. Retrieved April 13, 2023, from https://www.mckinsey.com/featured-insights/diversity -and-inclusion/women-in-the-workplace.

Hyatt, M. (n.d.). *How to Better Control Your Time by Designing Your Ideal Week.* Full Focus. Retrieved April 13, 2023, from https://fullfocus.co/ideal-week/.

Johns Hopkins. (n.d.). *Center for Psychedelic & Consciousness Research.* Center for Psychedelic & Consciousness Research. Retrieved April 13, 2023, from https://hopkinspsychedelic .org/.

Lama, D. (2009). *The Art of Happiness, 10th Anniversary Edition: A Handbook for Living.* Riverhead Books.

LaPorte, D. (2014). *The Desire Map: A Guide to Creating Goals with Soul.* Sounds True.

Leiter, M. P., & Maslach, C. (1999). Six areas of worklife: a model of the organizational context of burnout. *J Health Hum Serv Adm, 21*(4), 472–489. National Library of Medicine. https://pubmed.ncbi.nlm.nih.gov/10621016/.

Maier, S.F., & Seligman, M.E. (1976). Learned helplessness: Theory and evidence. *Journal of Experimental Psychology, 105*(1), 3–46. APA PsycNet. https://doi.org/10.1037/0096-3445.105.1.3.

Maslach, C., Jackson, S. E., & Leiter, M. P. (1997). Maslach Burnout Inventory: Third edition. *Evaluating stress: A book of resources,* 191–218. APA PsycInfo. https://psycnet.apa.org/record/1997-09146-011.

Mayo Clinic. (n.d.). *Job burnout: How to spot it and take action.* Mayo Clinic. Retrieved April 13, 2023, from https://www.mayoclinic.org/healthy-lifestyle/adult-health/in-depth/burnout/art-20046642.

McGregor, J. (2021, October 19). Sabbaticals Are on the Rise to Help Retain Workers. *Forbes.* Retrieved April 14, 2023, from https://www.forbes.com/sites/jenamcgregor/2021/10/19/sabbaticals-are-on-the-rise-to-help-retain-workers-can-they-battle-burnout/?sh=b6ee9ac23f76.

Montero-Martin, J., & Garcia-Campayo, J. (2010). A newer and broader definition of burnout: Validation of the "Burnout Clinical Subtype Questionnaire (BCSQ-36)." *BMC Public Health, 10*(0), 302. https://doi.org/10.1186/1471-2458-10-302.

Moore, A., & Malinowski, P. (2009). Meditation, mindfulness and cognitive flexibility. *Conscious Cogn., 18*(1), 176–86. National Library of Medicine. https://pubmed.ncbi.nlm.nih.gov/19181542/.

Nagoski, E., & Nagoski, A. (2019). *Burnout: The Secret to Unlocking the Stress Cycle.* Ballantine Books.

Neuroplasticity—HOPES Huntington's Disease Information. (2010, June 26). HOPES Stanford. Retrieved April 13, 2023, from https://hopes.stanford.edu/neuroplasticity/#strategies-for-promoting-brain-reorganization.

Pollan, M. (2019). *How to Change Your Mind: What the New Science of Psychedelics Teaches Us About Consciousness, Dying, Addiction, Depression, and Transcendence.* Penguin Books.

Schabram, K., Bloom, M., & DiDonna, D. (2023, February 22). *Research: The Transformative Power of Sabbaticals.* Harvard Business Review. Retrieved April 13, 2023, from https://hbr .org/2023/02/research-the-transformative-power-of -sabbaticals.

Sharif, M.A., Mogilner, C., & Hershfield, H.E. (2021). Having too little or too much time is linked to lower subjective well-being. *Journal of Personality and Social Psychology, 121*(4), 933–947. APA PsycNet. https://doi.org/10.1037/pspp0000391.

Singer, M. A. (2007). *The Untethered Soul: the journey beyond your-self.* New Harbinger Publications.

Wiest, B. (2020). *The Mountain Is You.* Thought Catalog Books.

Yielder, P., & Li, T. (2017, July 30). *Exercise Promotes Neuroplasticity in Both Healthy and Depressed Brains: An fMRI Pilot Study.* Neutral Plasticity. Retrieved April 13, 2023, from https://doi .org/10.1155/2017/8305287.

Zhu, M. (2018, February). *The Mere Urgency Effect | Request PDF.* ResearchGate. Retrieved April 14, 2023, from https://www .researchgate.net/publication/327103488_The_Mere_Urge ncy_Effect.

About the Author

Laura Nguyen is an experienced marketing executive and entrepreneur with an extensive background in data-driven marketing, digital marketing and communications for Fortune 500 companies. With two decades of corporate experience, she has led high-performing teams to achieve organizational growth and market share dominance. She is the founder of Solle Solutions, a marketing consultancy. Laura is also a certified executive coach, helping midcareer, high-achieving leaders go from burned out to balanced through her coaching program and online community.

Laura received her bachelor of arts and bachelor of science degrees from Truman State University, and her MBA from Rochester Institute of Technology. She lives in Des Moines, Iowa, with her family.

"My mission in life is not merely to survive, but to thrive; and to do so with some passion, some compassion, some humor, and some style."

—Maya Angelou